31st December 1995

Dear loor

To wish you a most
special 70th birthday
Much love

Gay
xx

Swings and Roundabouts

GRAHAM DILLEY
AND GRAHAM OTWAY

Swings and Roundabouts

Best Regonds

Graham Otway

PELHAM BOOKS

First published in Great Britain by
Pelham Books Ltd
27 Wrights Lane
London W8 5TZ
1987

British Library Cataloguing in Publication Data

Dilley, Graham
    Swings and roundabouts: the autobiography
    of Graham Dilley.
    1. Dilley, Graham   2. Cricket players——
    England——Biography
    I. Title   II. Otway, Graham
    796.35'8'0924   GV915.D5

ISBN 0-7207-1795-7

Typeset by Quorn Selective Repro, Leicestershire.
Printed and bound in Great Britain by
Butler and Tanner, Frome, Somerset.

Contents

Foreword

This book owes its inception and probably much of its inspiration to several late night beers in a Melbourne Piano Bar as England celebrated winning the Ashes in Australia. The flow of conversation was constantly interrupted by a series of Aussies seeking an autograph or merely saying 'Well done, even if you are a Pom'.

After so much TV and press coverage of the Ashes Down Under it was almost impossible to step anywhere without being recognised. That had not always been the case during an England career that had suffered from fits and starts since it began, also in Australia, in the winter of 1979. In the years that followed small triumphs were often followed by a loss of form or, worse still, injury and the critics were often quick to seize upon the latter.

After early hiccups for the whole team the 1986–87 Australian tour turned out to be one of the most successful in the history of English cricket. To have been a member of the touring party was an honour in itself, to be a member of an all-conquering England side, after so many previous disappointments, was extra special.

Throughout my career many words have been written about Graham Dilley but few of them have come from me. I hope this book will explain the feelings and thoughts, motives and even the injuries that have shaped my career. It was never intended to be just a record of my every ball bowled in first class cricket or every wicket taken.

When I was at Kent we had a saying in the dressing room for anything in a match which didn't go quite according to our plans. Deleting the expletives it could be shortened to 'Swings and Roundabouts' – hence the title.

Graham Dilley
Worcester, June 1987.

1

The New Boy

I was young and it all happened so fast. Some said later it was maybe too fast for my own good, but whatever the verdict my rise from the ranks of club cricket in Kent to being a fully fledged England fast bowler was certainly meteoric. It had always been a driving ambition to play for my country, even so to be chosen to take part in a full tour to Australia at the age of twenty was beyond my wildest childhood dreams.

It was an exciting venture and not totally unsuccessful, but it was to take another eight years before I could finally wake up each morning and say I had become an established member of the England team. In the intervening years there were to be moments when I thought I had made it and other times when perhaps I should have made it. There were moments of brief elation but many of deep despair – mainly with injuries of which I was to experience far more than my fair share. But that also is moving ahead too fast.

The selectors clearly took a huge gamble early in the September of 1979 when they pencilled me into the 'kiss and make up' tour that was arranged after an armed truce had been declared with Kerry Packer. Since there were only to be three Tests played the Ashes were not put up for grabs but the matter or prizes meant little to me. I had a chance of playing for England and that was enough.

Such thoughts had been cherished from the earliest days when my father and brother Brian first let me hold a bat as little more than a toddler on Dartford Heath and through my school days. By the age of fifteen I was knocking on the window of Kent coach Colin Page's car, in the car park at Dartford Cricket Club and begging for advice on a cricketing career. Despite his assistance at Saturday morning nets I had to take a job as a diamond setter in Hatton Garden on leaving school, though I was quick to discard the £20 a week wages when forced to make a choice between work and playing midweek games for Kent seconds.

For two winters I built up my strength humping huge sheets of plasterboard for an uncle's office partitioning firm and just waiting for the summers when I could pick up £5 a day plus expenses with Kent and play in the League for Dartford at the weekend. Cricket was by then my life and my realistic aim in my late teens was to breakthrough into the Kent side. I made my first class debut at Cambridge University in 1977, but I must have been very naïve – I remember being impressed by the batting prowess of Kevin Jarvis when he hit a six and he was to become one of the world's most confirmed number elevens. A year later I was at Lord's for my Championship debut against Middlesex, taking 5 for 32 in their second innings, but far too nervous and overawed to take in the full majesty of the place.

Barely twelve months later I was on a plane for Australia after the selectors had decided to hand over a set of air tickets to a complete rookie. I had played just about one full season in the Kent first team, had no experience of overseas conditions apart from county tours to play club sides in Canada and the West Indies and had never lived away from my parents' home.

In the *Boy's Own* comic a youngster first selected for his country would hear the news in some exciting setting – for me it arrived in the car park at the St Lawrence Ground, Canterbury. It was the last night of the season and we had been playing Middlesex, led as usual by Mike Brearley who was to captain England that winter. Brearley had asked Derek Underwood to have a quiet word with me and the opportunity arrived as I stowed my gear away in my car before heading for an end of term function.

Underwood said simply 'We are going mate,' and I honestly thought he was referring to the pub and a quick pint. When he mentioned the word Australia I could only stare at him open mouthed in disbelief. I had not had an outstanding first season in the Kent side taking only forty-six first class wickets in twenty matches and that was chicken feed when compared to other contenders for a tour place like Robin Jackman who had taken one hundred and twenty wickets in 1979 and there were other candidates with eighty or ninety each. But the selectors had made their choice and I was going to make the most of it,

Early international honours – bowling for England against the West Indies in the 1978 Agatha Christie Under 19 Test series. (*Patrick Eagar*)

10

particularly the opportunity to play under Brearley.

Having heard so much said on television and radio about Brearley and read numerous articles on the man I had tremendous respect for him even before we met. It was said that he was the best captain England ever had and I never saw anything later which shattered that belief. For Kent I had played under two men – Asif Iqbal, so inspirational for Pakistan but by then weary of the day to day grind of the county circuit, and Alan Ealham, a jovial 'up and at 'em' type but who gave me the impression that enjoying one's cricket was far more important than actually winning.

Playing for Brearley was to be an education and I was awestruck. He would work everything out before a match began. Although we lost that winter's series to the Aussies three-nil and things did not go exactly as he planned Brearley went through the same routine of scheming the games and deciding how to extract the best out of an individual to make things work the way he wanted.

Brearley always liked to have a talk with his players before the start of the match. I had been used to just turning up at a ground, loosening up and then getting on with the job in hand. No one had ever tried to motivate me in county cricket, certainly not in three-day games and suddenly I was confronted with a captain who not only spoke to me early in the morning but also came and had a chat whenever necessary while I was bowling. He liked to involve me in fielding changes which I appreciated since there is nothing worse for a bowler than to turn at the start of his run and discover the field has been changed without warning.

Brearley's pre-match talks were never dogmatic and he never actually told me off, it was more often constructive criticism though he very much believed that if a player was good enough to represent England he should have been able to work out his own problems. He was perceptive enough, however, to know that some people needed more guidance than others.

On that first trip to Australia he also made sure that other people did not try to influence England's young fast bowling find and he felt I needed protection particularly from Fred Trueman who was working as a broadcaster for Channel Nine that winter. During the summer Trueman had been to watch me in action at Tunbridge Wells and told Underwood to pass on the message that he would be willing to have a chat with me at the end of the day's play. I traced Trueman to a sponsor's tent but it seemed impossible to have a proper conversation in that environment and I made an excuse and left bitterly disappointed. I would like to think that in a similar position if anyone was desperate enough to seek my advice I would make sure I could make some valuable comments.

Brearley had his own troubles on that Australian tour and I admired the dignified way in which he coped. His headache stemmed from the failure of the Test and County Cricket Board and the Australians to agree the tour playing conditions before we left London. Once in Australia, disagreements became public as Brearley together with TCCB chairman George Mann and tour manager Alec Bedser attempted to thrash out an agreement with the Aussie Board and the local crowds and press took the opportunity to give our captain as much stick as possible.

Matters came to a head in one of the early day/night games against the West Indies at Sydney when they wanted four to win off the last ball. We had refused to agree to the introduction of a thirty-yard restriction on fielders as, unlike the Australians and West Indians who had played under Packer, we had no experience of the tactics involved. So Brearley, well within the rules, sent everyone including wicket-keeper David Bairstow back to the boundary, we won the game and the crowds never forgave him after that.

Some volatile captains might have responded to all the taunts with a 'V' sign or similar gesture but for ninety-five per cent of the time Brearley was totally unruffled. Once, later in Sydney, I saw he was plainly upset but it soon passed over and he went back to being his normal self. The fact that at times the pressure did get through to him proved that he was human but his self control only served to increase my admiration of the man.

He needed to show patience with me, however, since my preparations for that tour had been almost laughable. In the two months between the end of the season and the trip beginning I had simply no idea how to prepare myself physically or even the type of kit I should pack. Underwood was the one Kent player who might have been able to give me advice as we met for the odd game of golf but the fitness needs of a spinner and those of a young fast bowler are world's apart.

I had watched Underwood's early morning warm-up with fascination for most of the summer – a quick cup of coffee and a cigarette and he was raring to go. I became convinced that the odd mile and a half of road running would get me by, but that idea quickly fell apart when we began our early tour nets in Sydney and I discovered that while I was physically fit because of my age I had not got the stamina for the rigours of a tour or for a five day Test match.

It really hit me hard when, after playing and doing well in most of the early games against state opposition, I was included in the side to face Australia in the first Test at Perth. I had been used to the County Championship where in those day there was a maximum hundred over limit on first innings. Even then I used to regard that as something of an ordeal, but there had always been the comforting feeling at the back of my mind that even if Kent lost the toss and we were forced to spend the first day in the field there would still be thirty to forty-five minutes near the end of the day when, as a bowler, I could have a bath and a beer and just relax while the openers began our reply.

Suddenly in Perth it dawned on me that if Australia batted first I could still be in the field two and a half days later. That was going through my mind when Dennis Lillee appeared at the wicket with his now famous aluminium bat and Brearley lodged his subsequent complaints with the umpires. On the issue with the bat and its legality I had no strong feelings either way but play was held up for fifteen minutes and I was just relieved to take the weight off my feet and sit down on the outfield. I was absolutely exhausted without the safety valve of the hundred overs which had been part and parcel of my games at county level up to that point.

Apart from fitness I was also at a loss about my behaviour. My chief memory of the seemingly endless flight from Heathrow was seeing Big Bob Willis go straight up to the stewardesses as soon as we got on board and talk his way into a seat with more room for his long legs. For a senior pro that was probably acceptable behaviour but as the newcomer and easily the youngest member of the party I did not dare follow suit and I was sentenced to twenty-six very uncomfortable hours in the air. Not being a good flier at the best of times, I had normally helped myself to sleep with a few tots of the hard stuff, but I refrained on that occasion because I did not want to be seen doing the wrong thing while proudly wearing my England blazer.

Apart from staying wide awake I was also lonely. With the exception of Underwood I knew hardly anyone else in the tour party although I had faced just a few of the other players in county games the previous summer. My natural reticence to make conversations with strangers did not help. I have never been outspoken when meeting people for the first time, preferring to sit back and watch and take everything in. I spent the whole flight doing that and trying to discover exactly where I

14

would fit into the scene. The others were all busy taking the mickey out of each other, which I was to learn later was normal tour behaviour, but at the time it seemed a very peculiar existence.

It was not that I thought that I should not be on the tour, but just being a part of the England side had come as a big shock to my life and I needed time to adjust to it all. It was only during the first week in Sydney that I began to feel more at ease and the turning point came during a game of hand football with the other lads. Brearley came over, put a hand on my shoulder and said 'Picca you'll be all right'. It may not have meant a lot to him or anyone who overheard the remark but to me that was the moment of my acceptance in the party.

But there was soon to come a time when my colleagues wanted as little to do with me as possible when it came to sharing hotel rooms. It all stemmed from a series of remarkable coincidences when my first room mate, Mike Hendrick, had to fly home early from the tour with an injury. He had hardly been gone two seconds, when Geoff Miller, installed in the bed alongside mine as a replacement, injured his back and was ordered home as well. After that the tour management made sure I kept well away from wicket-keeper Bob Taylor because they were scared I might complete a hat-trick of Derbyshire victims.

When the tour first began I thought my part in it would be fairly small – that I had been taken along to gain experience and would only play if one of the more experienced pacemen got injured – yet when I was picked to play in the first Test at Perth it came as no big shock. In the state games I had bowled well while Bob Willis was struggling to get his act together and John Lever had hardly figured at all. Naturally I was nervous leading up to my debut but Brearley was marvellous saying that I should just try to get the ball to the batsman as fast as possible and leave him to worry about the critics.

My first contribution as an England player came in the field and unfortunately the victim was an old mate Julien Weiner who had spent five months the previous summer staying with my family while playing second eleven cricket for Kent. Greg Chappell called for a single to me at mid-wicket and I ran Weiner out with a direct throw at the stumps. But my jubilation was quickly flattened as I experienced the Gorilla Hug for the first time. It came of course from Ian Botham who traditionally greets the taker of any wicket for England by grabbing the poor fellow around the chest and squeezing the air from his lungs. It's nice to be appreciated by one's colleague but it does not do the health any good. Still that is Botham all over and he would not

A rare wicket on my first tour to Australia as Rod Marsh departs after being bowled in a World Series Cup one-day game. (*Adrian Murrell*)

have been the same man or cricketer without his unbounding enthusiasm.

My first actual wicket was an all Kent affair as Peter Toohey hooked an attempted bouncer straight down Underwood's throat at long leg and also in the Aussies' first innings Bob Taylor dived down the leg side to catch Rod Marsh. When they batted a second time the scorebook recorded the famous poetical dismissal of 'Lillee c Willey b Dilley' and finishing with match figures of 3 for 97 from 36 overs was enough to earn me a second cap in the Sydney Test.

I moved on with runs as well as wickets under my belt having scored an unbeaten 38 in my first innings for England. It had proved to be a pretty painful affair since I was hit early on the forearm by a Jeff Thomson special that lifted quickly off the pitch. During that innings I was aware of repeated warnings that it would be tough in the middle against the Aussies with their reputation for 'sledging', particularly at young newcomers. In fact no one said a word to me, but it helped to have Bruce Laird, one of cricket's nice guys, fielding at short leg for he just let me get on with my job.

On the way to Sydney I reflected on my debut performance and I realised that it was not quite as tough as many people might have expected. Once the match had got underway there were hardly any nerves, probably because one's first Test, like one's first tour, is the easiest of them all. In most cases no one expects too much from a newcomer and anything that is produced is a bonus. In later years when I had a name to live up to and people had greater expectations I was to discover what the word pressure really meant.

Despite my early successes at Perth I failed to get a wicket in the second Test and was forced to miss the final match of the series after damaging the intercostal rib muscle during a one-day game. It also kept me on the sidelines for the Jubilee Test in Bombay which rounded off the tour. The end of tour averages later revealed that I had taken just seven first class wickets on the trip which drew a gasp of disbelief from tour manager Alec Bedser who said simply '**** me, seven thousand quid for seven wickets'.

But my first excursion with England was not a total disaster for me because as *Wisden* recorded later 'Unable to get a place in the Kent side at the start of the summer Dilley won a place in the Test team and, at times, looked faster than anybody on either side.' To me that seemed a huge compliment considering that some of the greatest fast bowlers in history – Dennis Lillee, Jeff Thomson and Bob Willis – took part in that series and I could never hold a grudge against Bedser for his remark because I could not have asked for a better man as my first tour boss.

Although he was a magnificent bowler in his day for Surrey and England Bedser never tried to influence me in any way in my development. One day in the nets on tour he did, and I think it was out of devilment, put down a white handkerchief on a length and tried to get all the bowlers to hit it. That was the sort of exercise Bedser had done in his own heyday and I do not think our efforts went down too well in his eyes, but he did not labour the point.

Over the years Bedser's critics accused him of being staid and slightly old fashioned in his views and urged that he stop seeing modern players through the eyes of someone who played his cricket in the 1940s and 1950s. But on a tour overseas with a pack of young, energetic and sometimes playful athletes it was not such a bad thing to have some sort of stable influence in the background.

As chairman of England's selectors, a role he held for thirteen years, Bedser always had a caring attitude towards his players and for my first three years as an England player I came into contact with him quite a lot. If he was down watching Kent he would always seek me out and have a quiet word. If I was doing badly he would tell me not to give up hope and to remember that I was still in the selectors' thoughts and if things were going well he encouraged me to try even harder and his support meant a lot.

In Bedser's day cricketers were never that well paid and he certainly thought that my £7,000 tour fee from the Test and County Cricket Board was a huge sum of money and it certainly made a difference to me. Before being picked for England I was uncapped at Kent and barely earned £2,000 a year. Suddenly when I returned to England I had money in the bank for the first time in my life. An old friend who had played with me at Dartford and was earning a living as an estate agent advised me, very wisely, to invest in a house of my own and before the new season back at home I was looking at property.

My elevated status as an England player also led to sponsors providing me with a brand new car. During my early seasons with Kent I had travelled from ground to ground in a battered, but souped up, Ford Capri which needed constant attention, but was all I could afford at the time. But by the start of the 1980 summer I was kitted out with a brand new Vauxhall Cavalier and with money in the bank, and soon my own house – a whole new world had opened up.

In Kent's committee room however, playing for England on a major tour to Australia seemed to cut no ice at all. Apart from my normal entitlement under agreements with the Professional Cricketers' Association, there was no increase in wages waiting for me when I reported back for pre-season training and I had to wait until halfway through the season before the county saw fit to award me my cap.

It was a bit of a bug with me and for the first time in my career, but certainly not the last, I found myself disagreeing with the county over money. I felt that if the selectors had considered me good enough to play for my country Kent should recognise the fact. Being honest with myself I knew I had not done a lot for the county at that stage since I had only taken around seventy first-class wickets. Although I did not know how much the other youngsters at the county were getting I felt underpaid, but one thing I did know was that Kent had no one else on their books at the time who could bowl with genuine pace and therefore I felt I should be considered as a valuable asset.

Finally a meeting was arranged with Arthur Phebey, the chairman of Kent's Cricket Committee and he tried to find a way of increasing my salary without upsetting the basic wage structure at the club. His first suggestion was to introduce a bonus scheme whereby I would be rewarded for the number of wickets taken for Kent each season, but I quickly ruled that out as a non-starter. My first reservation was because I would only start earning sizeable sums of money at more than eighty victims per summer and that did not seem a realistic possibility – firstly the wickets at Kent were never going to give sufficient assistance and furthermore if I was bowling that well I would be a regular in the England team and never play sufficient county games to pick up my bonus. I was also concerned that I would be the only player at Kent to benefit under the system and I had always believed in trying to help my team mates as well as myself.

After much discussion Kent finally came up with a system which would reward me for playing for England and the same conditions were to apply to the rest of the team. So by the time I had sorted out the money element the tour had clearly left me a damn sight better off. But there were drawbacks as well. As an England player I began to find a lot more pressure on me to perform every time that I took to the field and I was also in the public eye off the field for the first time. I had always considered myself a fairly quiet, home loving person and it was a strange feeling to be put under the microscope for the first time.

The fact that for the next decade most of my movements would be scrutinised struck home the following November as Helen and I made plans for our wedding. We had been introduced two years earlier by my Kent colleague Graham Johnson, who was married to her sister, but had only been going out for a year when we decided to tie the knot. I had no thoughts for anything else but a quiet, simple, family affair, but once news of the event leaked out I began to get a series of 'phone calls from papers in Fleet Street asking for interviews and photographs and I did not know how to handle it all.

As a result I made a real gaff and had my first serious run in with the press when a reporter from the William Hickey column on the *Daily Express* rang up and asked if they could send a cameraman along to the church. The 'phone call got quite heated and we reached an impasse with the paper wanting a picture and me insisting none should be taken. Finally, in desperation, I tried one last ploy to shake the guy off.

I said 'If you want the picture that badly ... how much?' It was the worst possible thing I could have said because instead of ending up with a picture of myself and Helen on our happy day the paper printed a damning story of me demanding money, and it did not stop there. Someone made a 'phone call to the Test and County Cricket Board at Lord's asking for their reaction and the next thing I knew I was asked to attend a meeting with Alec Bedser. Fortunately he took an understanding pose and after listening to my side of the story and all the reasons for my action he offered to support me publicly until all the furore died down. Fleet Street, however, is full of persistent men and after all the bad publicity our wedding day turned out to be anything but quiet since there was a pack of photographers present to record the event.

2

Caribbean Carnage

The picture postcards and holiday brochures that show palm-fringed beaches alongside a deep blue ocean paint a picture of the Caribbean which is idyllic for the holiday maker who wishes to go sun worshipping for a couple of weeks. Many of my close friends were deeply jealous when I was selected to tour the West Indies with England for three months at the start of 1981. Because this was my second trip I felt more streetwise and confident than I had before departing for Australia fifteen months previously.

Within a matter of weeks, however, my tune had changed dramatically and I would have given anything to be put on the next flight to England even though it was still midwinter and snow lay on the ground at home. For pleasure-seeking tourists the West Indian Islands may be the nearest thing to heaven on earth but for me, a professional cricketer, I found them very disappointing – providing in my experience the worst practice facilities of all the countries on the international Test circuit.

From my earliest days at Kent I had become used to facing the many West Indians who choose to earn a living playing county cricket. My first taste of them as international opponents had come in Australia when we met them in the first ever World Series Cup, but I really discovered at first hand what a mighty team they had become under the captaincy of Clive Lloyd in the summer of 1980 when they undertook a full tour of England.

Despite my relatively successful start in Test cricket down under I was overlooked for the opening clash of the summer at Trent Bridge which was Ian Botham's first as England's new captain. According to *Wisden* it was the match which marked the official healing of the rift caused in English cricket by the Packer Affair, and my Kent colleagues Allan Knott and Bob Woolmer were welcomed back into the international fold. But the homecoming was disappointing as

Ian Botham and I didn't always see eye to eye when he was England's captain.
(*Adrian Murrell*)

England lost a low scoring match on a difficult Nottingham pitch by two wickets.

Nevertheless as the West Indies chased only 208 for victory the England bowlers, led by a five wicket haul from Bob Willis, put up a tremendous fight and I was therefore mildly surprised to find myself included in the squad for the second Test at Lord's. It could have been quite a Test for Kent since Woolmer, Knott, Chris Tavare and Derek Underwood were also picked but sadly I was made twelfth man and the opportunity never arose again for me to be one of five players from our county to be selected by England in the same match.

My disappointment turned out to be shortlived since I made the side for the drawn third Test at Old Trafford and made a big impact on the

Faoud Bacchus about to depart caught at slip by Botham during the Old Trafford Test. (*Patrick Eagar*)

strong West Indian batting line. Although we made only 150 batting first, Willis and I had the West Indians in all sorts of trouble at 25 for 3. Big Bob started the rot by having Desmond Haynes caught behind, before I picked up my first wicket on English soil as Gordon Greenidge turned a ball into the hands of Wayne Larkins fielding at backward square leg. The very next ball Ian Botham took what I then regarded as the best catch I had seen in my short career.

I produced a slightly short lifting delivery outside the off stump which flew like a rocket off the shoulder of Faoud Bacchus' bat. Botham, as per usual, had his hands firmly planted on his thighs at slip, but in an instant he leaped high in the air, twisted and stretched out a hand to take the ball just as it seemed to have gone past him. With

Clive Lloyd delighting his adoring Lancashire public with his thirteenth Test century the West Indies earned a first innings lead of 110, but a total of ten and a half hours were lost to rain and we ended with a draw.

The weather also intervened at the Oval and Leeds, the venues of the fourth and fifth Tests, sentencing them both to stalemates much to the frustration of the paying public, but I at least emerged from both games with an enhanced reputation.

Again batting first at the Oval we made 370 after openers Graham Gooch and Geoff Boycott for once blunted the West Indian pacemen with a first wicket stand of 155. After the Saturday had been washed out and with Lloyd unable to bat because of a severely strained hamstring, we dismissed the West Indies for 265 thanks largely to my own contribution of 4 for 57 from twenty-three pretty mean overs. I picked up another four-wicket haul in the game at Headingley and for the first time, even though I was still only twenty-one, I felt totally at home in England colours and could contemplate having a long and hopefully successful career ahead of me.

My eleven wickets in the series had cost me just 16.63 runs apiece, and although John Emburey topped the English averages for the series, I came second with great names like Willis, Botham and Lever behind.

Within a matter of days, however, I was to learn for the first time, but certainly not the last, that a fast bowler should never count his chickens. Although I bowled well at Leeds, I had felt that something was not quite right with me when I reported before the match, but after my success in the previous two Tests I did not want to pull out of the game and my performances justified that decision. But there was definitely something wrong. I am normally a healthy eater with a big appetite but food just didn't appeal to me and I was finding it hard to swallow liquids.

By the end of the Test I felt completely exhausted and after a series of blood tests had been carried out doctors diagnosed that I had contracted a mild dose of glandular fever and ordered me to rest. It was a sickening blow because it meant that I had to miss the rest of the season and more importantly I was not available for the Centenary Test against Australia at Lord's which completed that summer's home international fixture. I would have dearly loved to have lined up alongside all the great names of Ashes cricket who assembled in London for the match instead of which I was forced to sit at home and watch it on television.

At full tilt against the West Indies at Headingley in the fifth Test. (*Patrick Eagar*)

The selectors took a bit of a gamble but certainly lifted my spirits early in September when they named the touring party for the West Indies and included me in it. I was fortunate in a way because had it been a tour to either India or Australia which traditionally begin early in October there would have been no way I would have been fit enough to take part. But since Caribbean tours never start before January I had plenty of time to recover, especially since I had not developed the worst symptoms of the illness which can lay people up in bed for six months at a time. Allowed to exercise by walking and even permitted the odd sortie to the pub for a pint I was well on the mend by the time five members of the tour party were summoned to Edgbaston for pre-tour fitness checks.

25

I was declared fit after running around Warwickshire's car park a couple of times and using a running machine – feats I could probably have achieved even when my fever was at its worst. Such a cursory check proved not to be enough for two other tourists, Bob Willis and Chris Old. Willis broke down with knee trouble and was forced to return home after breaking down prior to our first game in Trinidad while Old, although he completed the tour, bowled just 62.3 overs during our three month trek around the islands.

Some people may be surprised to read after my experience of that tour to the West Indies, where just about everything one could imagine could go wrong managed to do so, that I would be hesitant about returning to the Caribbean. In the early warm up games which were vital for everyone but even more important for me since I had not bowled a ball in anger since mid-August, we were badly hit by rain. And on the days put aside purely for net practice the facilities were, on occasions, not up to the standard required by a team preparing for a tough Test series. In St Vincent where we played a series of three one-day matches against the Windward Islands our assistant manager Ken Barrington refused to let me bowl more than a couple of deliveries in the rain affected nets fearing I might injure our batsmen even before they had a chance to tackle the West Indies fast bowlers. Barrington instead despatched me into the outfield and said I should try and find my rhythm bowling at the sightscreen and since it was made of brick there was little chance that I would do any damage there.

I had only taken two wickets in fifty-three overs by the time we arrived in Trinidad for the first Test and it would be true to say that my form and fitness were well undercooked. But my own worries were a small issue compared to the political storm that was raging on the Island. Somehow Trinidad always seems to come up with some sort of controversy during an England tour – in 1986 the protestors were out on the streets angry that England had included Graham Gooch, the captain of the South African rebels in the party.

Five years earlier, however, it was an internal squabble that was dominating the daily headlines. Ever since the West Indies had announced their squad for the match the Trinidadians had been furious at the selectors' decision to play Barbadian wicket-keeper David Murray ahead of his local rival and namesake Deryck Murray. The controversy was further fuelled by the decision of the local cricket authorities to remove one of Deryck's close relations from his job as secretary at the Port-of-Spain Oval.

Fearing that protestors might slip into the ground and sabotage the pitch, floodlights were erected around the square and a security guard, complete with a dog, was posted on duty during the night before the game. Somehow, however, during the early hours of the morning the electricity failed and with the guard mysteriously leaving his post for half an hour, intruders broke in and damaged the pitch covers. Since it rained fairly heavily overnight there were still some damp patches on the wicket when the game was scheduled to start.

The whole England camp was well aware that our players were not properly match fit and none of us was too perturbed about the delay, neither was Clive Lloyd who had often expressed his dislike of playing in Trinidad because of the volatile crowds. The local anger grew as the morning progressed not only because of the issue of the two Murrays but also because no public announcements were made about the damp patches which made the delay in bright sunshine even more puzzling for the spectators. When Lloyd and Botham went out to make one pitch inspection, bottles were thrown over the security fence and with a definite possibility of a riot the match was ordered to get underway long before several of us felt the conditions were right.

When play finally started more than three hours late I ran into trouble with an England captain for the first time. The West Indies, batting first, piled a mammoth 426 for 9 with Greenidge and Haynes putting on 168 for the first wicket and I was accused of wasting the new ball. It was later said I should have bowled around the wicket to try and make use of the worst wet spots which were on a line just outside the batsmen's leg stumps. But I protested that I was the youngest of the three pace bowlers in our side, still learning my trade and still short of rhythm through hardly any match practice, and I didn't want to make matters worse by departing from my normal run and bowling action. Deep inside, however, I was more than happy bowling 28 overs on an otherwise flat pitch and conceding just 73 runs.

On the rest day at Trinidad's upside down Hilton Hotel – the lobby is on the top floor and guests take lifts down a cliff face to their rooms – Botham told the press at a conference that 'heads would roll' if England failed to bat through the final three days to save the match. In the event we were soundly thrashed by an innings and 79 runs as Colin Croft ran through our batsmen in the first innings and Michael Holding in the second, and Botham was left with egg on his face. This was especially the case because it was his untimely stroke against Viv Richards midway through the final afternoon and two overs before the

Bowled by Colin Croft in the first Test at Port-of-Spain. (*Patrick Eagar*)

new ball was due which exposed our fragile tail to the West Indian pacemen, when we might just have clung on for a draw.

Our spirits were pretty low by the time we arrived in Guyana for the next leg of the tour, but if we thought the atmosphere in Trinidad was a bit too hot to handle we had merely flown from the frying pan into the fire. No sooner had we booked into the Pegasus Hotel than a team meeting was called at which we were told about the threats to our safety in Georgetown. We were strongly advised that we should not leave the hotel alone and if we went out in pairs to make sure we left our watches and wallets behind and not to venture out at all after dark. With armed guards everywhere we were virtual prisoners when the famous 'Jackman Affair' blew up.

Robin, despite taking 114 wickets for Surrey the previous summer, had not been named in the original tour party and had only just flown out to join us as a replacement for Willis. The Guyanese government, however, took exception to the fact that Jackman had been visiting South Africa, both as a player and privately, on and off for ten years

28

after marrying his South African-born wife Yvonne and wanted to deport him. While tour manager Alan Smith and local British Embassy officials worked like beavers to try and find a solution to the crisis we tried to make life as normal as possible but it was a tough task.

Quite simply no nets were available to us. It rained a lot and we had to make do with a hard-surfaced playground near our hotel, but I could not bowl on that because with my 'drag' the concrete simply scraped all the skin off my toes. We were also given the use of a local gymnasium for inside work but that was another disaster. We tried to keep fit with games of five-a-side soccer but the place was full of mosquitoes driven indoors by rain outside and few of us escaped unharmed while Graham Gooch was left with around a hundred bites on just one leg.

The political rows were still raging as we flew up country to Berbice for a one-day international which we lost by six wickets after being bowled out for a paltry 137. That was hardly a surprising result since we had all had enough of the rows and discomfort. Had Lord's decided to abandon the tour on the spot I would not have been sorry. Although conditions all over were depressing enough it occurred to me that whatever happened we were going to struggle to win a test and the

A hug from Mike Gatting after capturing Gordon Greenidge caught behind at Barbados. (*Adrian Murrell*)

whole trip was going to be miserable.

Smith and the Guyanese government officials were unable to reach agreement over Jackman, the second Test was cancelled and we were evacuated to Barbados while the authorities worked out whether the tour should be called off or continued on a revised schedule – the only good thing to come out of the whole affair was that it was fairly clear it would be a long time before another English side would visit Georgetown. I thought as we left the country that I had reached an all-time mental low but another bombshell was on its way.

News of Ken Barrington's sudden death from a heart attack overnight in the Barbados Holiday Inn came like a bolt out of the blue. The previous evening, the Friday of the Barbados Test, Helen and I had been out for a relaxing dinner and returned to find him in the bar with his wife Ann full of good humour and not a hint that he might be ill. I just felt numb the next morning when the 'phone rang to tell me he had died and by the time we got on the field a few hours later to stand for two minutes silence in his memory I, like most of the other guys had tears in my eyes.

Barrington had been the assistant manager on my first tour with England to Australia and I had learned quickly not only to respect and learn from his views on the game of cricket but also to enjoy his company away from the field. Although cricket had been his life for many years he was able to forget the game away from the field and relax at the end of the day. He was, of course, famous for his malapropisms, like the day he told the players to go 'through irrigation' on their arrival at Sydney Airport or his assertion that crash helmets had saved many 'fertilities' against fast bowling. Stories about Barrington abound but to me he was a lot more than just a funny man. He cared and fussed for his players like a brooding hen.

He was the ideal guy to help a player through a tough tour. At the end of a particularly bad session in the field he would be there in the dressing room ready to find the right words that would make me want to go and bowl again forty minutes later full of fire in the gut. I really did love the old guy and although he had a history of heart trouble I am convinced that he was killed by the massive pressure the team was under on that tour.

He felt deeply for each of his players and while up to that point of the tour none of the team had been seriously injured by the non-stop West Indies pace attack I know that he was worried stiff that before the trip was over someone might actually be seriously hurt. He shared all the hassles that seemed to follow England around day by day and sympathised with our problems.

I had always been able to relate closely with Barrington and his sudden and tragic death only served to deepen my own depression. Suddenly the one person I knew I could turn to for help had been taken away overnight and it left a massive void. From a cricket point of view I felt alone and pretty helpless in a foreign and hostile country.

Looking back, it is obvious that his death overshadowed everything else that happened in the Barbados Test which we lost by 298 runs but I did feel some pride in luring the great Viv Richards with a sucker's

'No, I'm not going to bowl at you we are here to play tennis.' At court with Sir Geoff in Guyana. (*Patrick Eagar*)

31

punch. Earlier in Berbice we had seen the back of him fairly cheaply with a mishit hook shot, so when he emerged to bat during the West Indies first innings we made a deliberate show of posting two fielders back deep on the leg side as he took guard and prepared to face first ball. He was clearly expecting to be greeted with a bouncer and his feet were totally out of position when I sent down a well pitched delivery which held its line. The result was an edge which was well caught by Botham at slip. We all wore beaming smiles as he walked dejectedly back to the pavilion with a duck by his name but as Richards possessed so much talent I doubted whether the move would work again in the series.

He certainly came after us looking for revenge in the second innings as he struck a brilliant 180 and again when we moved onto Antigua where he was playing in front of his adoring home crowd – if one day he should ever stand for Prime Minister on the island I am sure his popularity is such that he would be voted in with a landslide victory. Richards scored a brilliant 114 in Antigua but there was also one other batting performance that cannot be passed over without a mention. Having batted first we were in deep trouble when I strolled out to the crease as last man with Peter Willey at the other end on 69 not out.

I knew it was my job to hang around as long as I could but against their pacemen my chances were pretty minimal. They looked even slimmer early on when they thought I edged Michael Holding into the gloves of Murray but instead of heading straight back for safety I stayed around and the umpire refused Holding's appeal. I have always believed it is up to the batsman to decide whether he should 'walk' or not. With Willey trying to take as much of the strike as possible I helped him add 36 for the last wicket – contributing just 2 not out – as he went on to complete a brave century and England reached 271 all out. Although Richards' century gave the West Indies a lead of 197 on the first innings rain came to our aid on the fourth day and we escaped with another draw.

While the Antigua Test was a pretty quiet affair I was soon back in the headlines as we went to Jamaica for the final Test. The problem arose from the boots I had taken with me on tour which simply were not strong enough for the pounding they were given on the hard Caribbean pitches. During the West Indian innings in which I grabbed

A rare joke in the West Indies shared with their great skipper Clive Lloyd. (*Adrian Murrell*)

four wickets I was forced to leave the field for some repairs. With my own boots useless and out of commission I had scrounged a pair off Ian Botham, and much to his and my annoyance I shed my left heel. There was nothing else I could do but leave the field, to find a cobbler and have the heel screwed back into place. My absence, however, did not go unnoticed and next day in the papers there was the suggestion that England's leading young fast bowler had foolishly gone on tour with only one pair of boots. It simply wasn't true since I had several pairs, the problem was that they were not up to the job.

The Jamaican Test also ended in stalemate thanks largely to David Gower who battled through the last seven hours of the match for 154 not out to secure a draw after we had conceded a first innings lead of 157 and so we headed home to sighs of great relief. As our jumbo jet took off from Kingston we sang a chorus of the British Airways advertising theme 'We'll take good care of you' and knew that we were heading for home.

A year later *Wisden* reported 'It was in bowling that, as expected, England were outclassed. Dilley, still only twenty-one, continued his improvement.' I didn't know quite how to take that from the official history of the game. We were bound to be outclassed because when a Test side has three or four genuinely fast bowlers all trying to knock batsmen's heads off, there is no respite, no hiding place and constant pressure. England simply had no armoury with which to respond. At times I knew I was capable of bowling as fast as any of the opposition but it was an uphill struggle. Once Willis had flown home I was the only genuine quick bowler in a party of medium fast pacers and the West Indies batsmen knew that they were in no danger from pace at the other end. It was a syndrome I was going to have to get used to.

3

Changing Fortunes

Despite my deep misgivings about the West Indies in general I returned home for the 1981 Ashes Series against Australia pretty confident about my place in the England set-up and I could not quite understand why I was left out of the side for the three Prudential Trophy matches at the beginning of June. I believed I had been through a reasonably successful tour of the Caribbean particularly in the Tests and had played in one of the two one-day internationals in the winter. Though we lost the game in seven overs I had claimed the valuable wicket of Viv Richards while conceding only 23 runs. I could only conclude that the selectors had decided that I was going to figure in their Test team plans for the summer and were holding me back to give other people a go.

To be fair though I had a poor start to the summer with Kent and my form was to dog me for the following twelve months. The record books show that I was picked for the first Test against the Aussies at Trent Bridge and reading straight from the scorecard it would appear that I had a highly successful match taking 3 for 38 in their first innings and 4 for 24 in the second. But it was to be a peculiar summer and certainly at Nottingham and in the two Tests that followed the record books told a lie. In those three games I got a total of fourteen wickets, which was not a bad return, but I was bowling badly and it just so happened that on the odd occasion I managed to get the ball near the stumps I got a wicket and the figures flattered me.

The crowds certainly were not fooled as I continually fired the ball wide down the leg side or was so far outside the target of the off stump that batsmen did not have to play a shot and at Nottingham the reaction of the members led to me getting in trouble with Lord's for the first time. Fielding at long leg right underneath the Press Box at Trent Bridge I started to get a lot of verbal stick from the members in the area, which upset me. Being only twenty-two at the time I was still rather hot

Bowled by Rodney Hogg in the first Test at Trent Bridge against the 1981 Aussies.
(*Adrian Murrell*)

headed and their abuse upset me. I firmly believed that they had paid their money to watch cricket and not to have a go at the players. My frustration finally boiled over when I had Dennis Lillee caught by Paul Downton and I turned and raised one finger at the crowd. Although it was only mentioned in the odd press report of the day's play, and even then well down the page, the incident had not gone unnoticed in the corridors of power. I later received a letter from Donald Carr, the secretary of the Test and County Cricket Board and he told me in no uncertain terms that it was not the sort of behaviour England wanted to see from one her players in a Test match. Having cooled down by then I readily agreed and wrote a letter of apology to the selectors promising that it would not happen again.

Although the authorities were not too happy with me, apart from my wickets I had also made a contribution with the bat that impressed in some quarters by scoring 34 in England's first innings. The match report in *Wisden* later described that knock as 'further proof of the Kent fast bowler's aspirations to be a genuine all-rounder'. But I could not agree with the writer because it just so happened that on the day the conditions were right for my style of batting.

As a youngster playing with my family on Dartford Heath and later as a schoolboy I had harboured pretensions as a batsman, but by the time I had entered the professional game with Kent second eleven in my late teens those notions had disappeared. By the summer of 1981 I was a genuine tailender and if I did score runs against the Aussies it was more by luck than judgement. At Nottingham when I went to the crease Mike Gatting was batting well on his way to 52 and for most of the hour I spent with him at the crease I simply tried to push a single as early as I could in each over to give him the strike. When he departed and Bob Willis followed first ball there was only last man Mike Hendrick left to keep me company. At that stage I started to wind up with the bat since I knew that the innings was not going to last much longer – a couple of slogged fours at that stage was always going to be more useful than defending with the knowledge that my poles would be knocked over at any time. It was one of those days when the slogging came off as we added 26 for the last wicket but I do not deserve any credit for my stroke play and to suggest that I could have become an all-rounder was widely off the mark.

We lost the Test by four wickets and my form showed no improvement as the Australians followed me down to Canterbury for Kent's game against the tourists the following weekend. Although rain

One back for me trapping Kim Hughes lbw in their second innings. (*Patrick Eagar*)

interrupted the match I was only given five overs in which to try and put things right before reporting back to England at Lord's the following Wednesday.

As a match the second Test is best forgotten since the weather, as always seemed to happen at cricket's headquarters, played havoc with the first day and on a flat pitch there was never really a chance of a result. Ian Botham declared on the fifth day setting the Australians 232 to win in 170 minutes in a bid to level the series but Graeme Wood battled sensibly for 62 to seal the draw. I had bowled thirty overs in the Australian first innings, which was by far my longest piece of the action in any Test, taking 3 for 106 and I also picked up John Dyson and Kim Hughes in the Australians' second dig, but again I was not happy. It is a fast bowler's job to bowl with fire, line and length and by that stage of the season I had accepted that I was not among the top three or four in England when it came to accuracy. All I could try to do was keep plugging away and hope that one morning I would wake up and everything would be all right again.

The Lord's Test will be remembered more for years to come as the match which signalled the end of Ian Botham's reign as England's captain. He had suffered a tough twelve months in two series against the West Indies and up to that point there had been little suggestion that England's fortunes might change against the Australians. Possibly seeing the writing on the wall Botham found Alec Bedser and resigned at the end of the fifth day though it was later revealed that the selectors had already decided that he should be replaced.

In a way I was sorry to see Botham go. Although we had had our occasional differences away on tour the previous winter, as any player and captain could have, we had always been fairly good friends. That said I had always had my doubts about him being given the job in the first place in spite of his great achievements. Botham did not fit my idea of an England captain whom I felt should have been a lot older than his twenty-four years and also with a lot more experience as a county captain. I believe that doing the job day in and day out in the championship to be the best possible training ground for a captain at Test level. It was for that reason that I welcomed the selectors' decision to recall Mike Brearley for the rest of the summer even though he had made it plain that he had no wish to go on future England tours. He at least gave the selectors time to look around for a suitable replacement.

Botham's personal form with both the bat and ball had suffered during the previous year. It would be wrong to say it was the pressures of captaincy that got to him on the field, it was more away from the play that he struggled. In those last few months in charge I do not think he was ever able to relax and the tension must have got to him. While I could not see Botham as an ideal captain I had admired his technical knowledge of the game ever since I had first played alongside him. In Australia two years earlier I remembered him having a word with Geoff Boycott whom Botham felt was so committed to going onto the back foot as a first movement at the crease that he had begun to lose power in his driving. Botham sorted Boycott out then and while he was no longer going to be captain of England I hoped the selectors would find some way to keep him involved and to harness his deep knowledge in the future. Away on a tour for months at a time he could still have a role to play helping players who might be going through a bad trot.

As a player I felt Botham would soon bounce back from his disappointment at losing the captaincy, but I did not realise just how swiftly he would recouperate. It took just twenty-four hours and I was part of the Kent team that suffered after we had travelled straight from Lord's to Taunton for a Benson and Hedges Cup semi-final. Botham received a sympathetic ovation from his local fans and proceeded to tear into us with the ball taking two wickets in his first three overs without conceding a run. The wicket of Bob Woolmer was typical of the man's aggressive instincts. He knew only too well that Woolmer was one of the best hookers in the game at the time, but knowing it was such a risky shot decided to take him on. Botham dropped the ball in short, Woolmer played a pretty good shot really but Nigel Popplewell, fielding at long leg, took a diving catch and Botham's strategy had paid off. At some stage during the game I sought him out to say I was sorry he had lost his job, but I felt awkward as I could not find the right words to express my feelings. Still Botham was back and he made the Australians pay for the rest of the summer.

It has since become part of cricket's folklore that Botham rescued England from the dead at Leeds, scoring a brilliant 149 after we had been forced to follow-on and setting up an astonishing victory where the bookmakers were at one stage quoting 500 to 1 against our chances of success.

I played no mean part myself scoring 56 as Botham and I put on 117 for the eighth wicket having gone to the crease in our second innings with the score at 135 for 7 and 92 runs still needed to make the Australians bat a second time. But in the hours leading up to the match I had been filled with dread. My form was so bad that I could not have bowled a hoop downhill, my confidence was at its lowest ebb and while I desperately wanted to stay in the England side, I knew I should not have been picked.

As the Australians scored 401 for 9 in their first innings I took 2 for 78 as my strike rate continued to mask my inner torment. In the years since I have watched the video replay of that match time and again and it is astonishing how few deliveries I actually managed to bowl at the stumps. By the time I went out to bat in that historic second innings I knew deep down that for the time at least I was playing my last Test for England.

Early on that historic Monday there had been a lot of talk in the England dressing room about how we were almost certain to lose and how some players had already booked out of the team's hotel preparing for an early getaway. I had not booked out myself, not because I had some premonition that we were going to save the match or even win it, but I had not thought it was the right thing for me to do – with my place in jeopardy I did not want to be seen as having a defeatest attitude.

Take that ... (*Patrick Eagar*)

And that ... (*Adrian Murrell*)

And that – Hammering the Aussies in my innings of 56 at Leeds. (*Adrian Murrell*)

41

Botham was hardly striking the ball all over the place when I went out to join him, he was just pushing the ball around and seemed intent on a not out after his pair of ducks at Lord's – though it seemed out of character for him to start thinking about playing for his averages. We had a quick chat and he said that I was capable of playing as well as any batsman and that if the ball was there to be hit I should have a dart at it. As it turned out the ball was there to be hit more often than not even though the Australians tried the usual ploy of slanting the ball across the body of a left hander. All the time Botham helped me to relax with his presence at the other end. If I played and missed he was standing at the other end grinning, if I tried a really big heave and made no contact he would just lean on his bat and laugh out loud.

Although I was eventually bowled by Terry Alderman, Chris Old hung around while Botham unleashed his full repertoire of shots and on the final morning the Australians found themselves needing 130 for victory. It was then that it became clear to me that Mike Brearley had spotted quickly the troubles I was having with the ball. He knew he could only bowl me at the start, hoping that my record that summer of striking an early blow would continue. There was clearly no way he could afford to bowl me for long if I was going to go for five runs an over. In the event I bowled two overs for 11 runs, failed to breakthrough and left the field with a thigh strain. Bernie Thomas told me it was not too serious and I went back on the field but by then I had already sent down my last delivery of the series.

Even though Bob Willis' eight wickets helped to bring about an astonishing eighteen-run England victory, I was surprised that the selectors decided to keep me in the squad for the fourth Test at Edgbaston. In the event I threw my shoulder out playing for Kent against Derbyshire and was forced to pull out of the game. Mike Brearley however had a word and explained that I would not have played anyway and had merely been named in the twelve because the selectors did not want to break up a winning side.

From that point the season rapidly went downhill. Because I had been involved in the first three Tests my heart was still with England during the last three and I watched with interest as Paul Allott came in for the first Test at Old Trafford and had quite a debut in front of his home crowd by taking a couple of early wickets and scoring 52 not out. But all the time I was struggling with Kent and by August I had been dropped down into the second XI. I do not blame the county for that – I was not even worth a place in the Kent side, but it still came as a bit of a shock when only weeks earlier I had been enjoying the Test match stage.

A bigger shock was in store for me when in September I was included in the party to tour India and Sri Lanka and I could only think that England's new captain Keith Fletcher had a large say in that. I had first met him on Kent's tour to the West Indies in the late seventies when Fletcher and John Lever had been invited along as guest players.

Fletcher and I got on well even though it was only a ten-day trip and he was someone I looked forward to meeting up with on the county circuit. I can only think now that he must have formed a good impression of me and had decided that I would be his man for India. It must have been a captain's choice, though he never said anything directly to my face, because on the basis of my performances against the Australians I should not think I was included in the lists of any of the other selectors. Kent's immediate reaction was to recall me for the final championship match of the season against Worcestershire at Canterbury, but the game was heavily restricted by rain and the eight overs I bowled gave no indication that Fletcher's gamble would pay off in the months that were to follow.

While I had been full of dreamy expectations for the Caribbean the previous winter I was under no illusions of the conditions I could expect to find on the sub-continent and the culture shock did not take long to strike home. As soon as the door of our Air India jumbo opened at Bombay in the early hours of the morning a pungent smell hit me. It was of fires built out of dried cow dung and incense and in the three and a half months that followed it never went away.

India is such a mixture. In the main Test centres we were put up in five star hotels that would rank alongside the best anywhere in the world but in other places we were forced to stay in conditions that defied belief and nowhere was that better illustrated than in Nagpur where we played our second game of the tour against the Indian Cricket Board President's XI.

Some Indians joke that Nagpur is situated virtually equidistant from Bombay, Delhi and Calcutta because if they moved it any closer to an individual city there would be loud complaints. But we arrived to find that there was no hotel in existence and for four days we would have to make do with a government rest house used to accommodate low grade civil servants visiting the town on business. The complex consisted of one main administration building and a series of bungalows set among palm trees. The bungalows were mosquito infested, rats kept popping up out of the sewage system and the only place set aside for our meals was a hastily erected tent.

It was under that canvas that I witnessed one of the typical exchanges regarding food that made the tour so difficult. One morning at breakfast, tired of the endless plates of fried eggs that had become our staple diet, John Lever asked the head waiter if it would possible to have an omelette. The chef was duly summoned and after a conversation in Urdu which none of us understood he rushed away muttering the word omelette on his breath. Five minutes later the chef reappeared empty handed and again had a long discussion with the waiter and again the only word we could make out was omelette. Needless to say five minutes later the chef returned with two fried eggs for an exasperated England fast bowler.

To be fair to most of the Indians we met, they bent over backwards to try to see that we got the best of everything, but in a country with limited resources the best is not always good enough, and we learned quickly never to send back any food because there was always a long gap between meals and there was no guarantee that whatever was served later would be any better.

India does, however, foster a good spirit among touring teams. With nowhere to go at night and virtually no choice of entertainment far greater use was made of the communal team room on that tour and most of us developed a taste for whisky. The Indian beer was not popular since it contained a lot of glycerine which tended to have a rather nasty effect on the bowels, but whisky, we had been advised, helped kill stomach germs, though only if taken in moderate quantities. Apart from the team room much time was spent lying on beds listening to music or slipping away to find a snooker table. India is where the game was invented and several tables can be found in the old colonial clubs which still exist despite the country's independence.

After a two week journey up country playing at Nagpur, Pune and Baroda we returned to Bombay for the first Test and while I was still struggling with my bowling I was surprised to find myself back in the England team. Again I got among the wickets finishing with 4 for 47 but it was still more by luck than judgement. Although I dismissed Dilip Vengsarkar with the new ball, my other three victims were all tailenders, including Dilip Doshi – a real ferret if ever there was one (ferrets always go in after the rabbits).

Again the figures may have looked impressive to an outsider but I was still in trouble and the realisation of how bad it was struck me one

Autograph hunters around the pool at Taj Mahal in Bombay. (*Patrick Eagar*)

day in the outfield. I was nearly in tears because with at least two and a half months of the tour to go I knew there was no way that I was going to be able to play a vital part. I could not bowl, there was no help in the wickets to give me any sort of confidence and on the odd occasion when I managed to get one straight and hit a batsman on the pads the chances of him being given out by the umpires in that series were virtually nil.

I never fully understood why I was kept in the side for the second Test at Bangalore and my bowling reflected my form when I took 0 for 75 as the Indians put the match well out of reach scoring 428 on the back of 172 from their captain Sunil Gavaskar who was at the crease for 11 hours and 48 minutes, the longest innings played in a Test by an Indian. Our problems stemmed from batting slowly in our first innings and it caused me to have a minor disagreement with Fletcher. Our top ordermen had taken their time at the crease, but when Bob Taylor and I tried to play sensibly late on while building a partnership of 69 for the ninth wicket, a message came out from the captain at the drinks interval that we should get a move because he wanted to declare. It all seemed a bit silly to me because if the recognised batsmen could not score at a pace to get us into a strong position I did not see why the tail enders should have been expected to.

'All right lovely boy.' Captain Keith Fletcher and I as characters from *"It ain't 'alf Hot Mum"* at the Christmas party in Delhi. (*Adrian Murrell*)

By the Christmas period when we played the third Test at Delhi, quickly to be followed by the fourth at Calcutta I was out of the side and generally at odds with everything. As the Indians concentrated on preserving their lead, earned in Bombay, the cricket became painful to watch and the tedium was only relieved by a new talking point when Geoff Boycott quit the tour at the end of the Calcutta Test. I could not understand the Yorkshireman's attitude. It has been mooted that he had merely gone on the tour with the sole intention of breaking Gary Sobers' world record of 8,032 Test runs and once that had been achieved did not want to know any more.

I was well aware that Boycott had a medical condition that was not quite suited to Indian conditions, but had I had his money and ability I would not have gone on the tour in the first place. He should have stayed at home and backed himself to break the record the following summer instead of causing a certain amount of disruption on tour.

Boycott certainly managed to upset a number of us by going off to play golf at the Tollyganj Club while supposed to be ill in bed during the Calcutta Test – if he was fit enough to stroll around the golf course he was fit enough to join the rest of us who were not actually playing in the Test and do his share of twelfth man duties. The sin was actually compounded when he called into the dressing room and asked if anyone cared to join him on the course.

The tour management's decision that Boycott should return was kept from us all as we boarded a train at Calcutta station for the journey into the steel manufacturing centre of Jamshedpur – India's equivalent of Scunthorpe – for the match against East Zone. Since a couple of other players were missing the game and spending the time resting at Fisherman's Cove, just outside Madras which was to be the venue for the fifth Test, no one really noticed Boycott's absence. The story only filtered through later that night causing much consternation among our band of travelling journalists who discovered that all telex lines from Jamshedpur closed down at 11 p.m.

Some were still desperately trying to get copy out when the match started the next morning on the first green wicket we had seen all winter. Graham Gooch who was filling in for Fletcher as captain, gave Allott and myself extensive workouts as we bowled 55 overs between us and shared eight wickets while East Zone were dismissed for 242. It was nice to get some response from the pitch but we knew that Madras would do us no such favours. Our batsmen opted for practice rather than trying to get a result in the match and by the final day another dull draw was on the cards. During the East Zone second innings Allott and I were reduced to impersonating Derek Randall in the field to keep us occupied and the spectators amused while Gooch went through his comic routine of imitating the actions of England bowlers and inadvertently put himself in the record books.

The Essex opener was called for 'throwing' as he deliberately accentuated John Emburey's quicker ball – he did not know at the time that during England's innings East Zone's Kamal Das had been called for throwing as well, thus making an otherwise unremarkable match the only first class game in history where two bowlers had their actions questioned by the umpire. Obviously since Gooch was only fooling around the legitimacy of the record must be queried.

Although I had finally got some wickets in Jamshedpur my selection to play in the Madras Test was based more on my batting performances earlier in the tour. Fletcher and his co-selectors had decided that England's only hope of drawing level in the series was to play an extra bowler at the expense of a batsman and since I had scored 52 in Bangalore he decided I was quite capable of batting at number seven in

LEFT: 'Isn't it about time you went?' Trying to get the message through to Gundappa Viswanath during his innings of 222 at Madras. (*Adrian Murrell*)

OPPOSITE: A rare ball above head height in India as a bouncer roars past Pronob Roy at Madras. (*Adrian Murrell*)

the order. The move failed on two accounts since Gundappa Viswanath scored 222 and Yashpal Sharma 140 on a flat track as the Indians piled on 481 for 4 declared. With Vengsarkar having earlier scored 71 before being forced to retire hurt after being struck by Willis, we actually spent ten and a quarter hours in the field without getting a wicket. To put that into perspective one Indian journalist noted that the population of his country had actually risen by 75,000 during that time. Thanks to 127 from Gooch we easily fought our way through for a draw though my own batting failed to live up to all expectations since I made only 8 before popping up a return catch to Kapil Dev.

My batting helped me retain my place for the final Test at Kanpur, which at least gave Helen, who had flown out for a holiday, a chance to see me in action. The circumstances however were not the best as rain and bad light ensured that there was never going to be enough playing time for us to get a positive result and in 14 overs I conceded 67 runs – finishing that leg of the tour as I had started and that was not knowing where the ball was going when it left my hand. Still I did help David Gower get his first Test wicket as the match was drawing to a close by catching Kapil Dev at square leg after the Indian equivalent of Ian Botham had smashed his way to 116.

Our travels that winter ended in Sri Lanka where the first Test match between the two countries was scheduled to be played and while Fletcher finally got the Test victory he so desperately wanted as England's captain, I played no part at all. While England's spinners were setting up a seven-wicket win. With approval I spent most days on the beach with Helen and Gatting and his wife Elaine. It was probably the best thing I could have done at the time. It had been nearly twelve months since I had bowled a respectable spell and having tried various methods to put things right a break from cricket was a last resort.

There had been times, particularly towards the end of the previous summer, when my lack of form had begun to depress and I seriously began to question my future in the game. It was at its worst when I found myself playing for Kent second eleven only weeks after playing in an Ashes Series which is surely the pinnacle of cricket. Although I had not sought out anyone for advice I was given plenty during that lean year, some of it helpful, some of it not. It hurt me most when people suggested that my action was the root of many injuries since apart from dragging my back foot I basically bowled the ball like anybody else. Changing my action just to avoid getting injured might have led to a complete destruction of what talent I had.

At the end of the tour I heard on the grapevine that Raman Subba Row, the manager, had not submitted a very favourable report about me to Lord's but I could not see how I was to blame since the selectors had sent me on tour at a time when I was bowling well below my best and the conditions in India had done nothing to help me pull through. I could only imagine that he had not been impressed on the long train journey back from Jamshedpur when I sat at the back of the carriage and drank a whole bottle of Kahlua along with a couple of other players and I have to confess we got slightly drunk. I accept it was not the behaviour expected of an English cricketer on tour, though Subba Row said nothing to me at the time. It was just a minor indiscretion and not one that I felt should be left as a total indictment of my attitude towards the trip as a whole.

4

Oh for Hindsight

Taking the wrong turn at a vital crossroads in life is a simple error that can befall anyone, but the more I look back to the winter of 1981–82 the more I realise that my decision to pull out of the 'Rebel' England tour to South Africa was financially costly. Had I joined the other fifteen players who went on the month long trip I would have been forced to serve a three-year ban from Test cricket like the rest and been the subject of much heated debate which at its height reached the House of Commons.

Both Helen and I would have been put under intense pressure but as it turned out the tour would have given me far greater financial security than I was to achieve staying within the legal framework of the game. For while the rebels spent three years in international exile but with money in the bank I too was mainly out of the England team suffering from a series of injuries and loss of form, with only my county salary to fall back on.

My connections with the rebels stretched back to the very earliest days of the project when my interest in going was keen. The initial talks on the tour were strictly between Geoff Boycott, who had been visiting South Africa regularly for years, and Peter Cooke an entrepreneur from Johannesberg and a close friend of the Yorkshire and England batsman. But I was to be one of the five original players that were taken into their confidence as soon as they decided to turn their idea into reality.

The timing of Boycott's decision to sound out other players could not have been more ironic as he chose the Pegasus Hotel in Georgetown for our first meeting just as the 1981 tour to the West Indies was in danger of falling apart over the Guyanese government's decision to deport Robin Jackman because of his strong South African connections. Heaven alone knows what the Guyanese would have done had they found out that Boycott, Ian Botham, David Gower, John

Waiting for the outcome of the Jackman Affair in Guyana with the central character in the drama and John Emburey. (*Patrick Eagar*)

Emburey, Graham Gooch and myself were sitting in a hotel room under the noses of their security men giving birth to a project that was to cause an even greater furore in the cricketing world just over a year later.

Boycott had very few details of the tour available at our first meeting. He was basically bouncing ideas off us all to try to discover whether the concept of sending a strong side of internationals to South Africa was a feasible proposition, but he did let on that Holiday Inns had been approached and declared their willingness to put up the money for the tour.

It took no time at all for us to agree with Boycott that arranging a

52

tour would be possible, though deep down we all must have known that a party of England cricketers visiting South Africa, whether it be under a national banner or merely as a group of individuals was likely to cause tremendous shockwaves. I knew very little at the time about the Gleneagles Agreement, which was to be so widely quoted in the following months, but any tour of the nature proposed was bound to upset both the Test and County Cricket Board and the Government. The size of the pay cheques players could expect was not discussed in Guyana nor were dates but Boycott asked us all to sign a letter declaring our interest in the scheme. It was never intended to be a binding contract or a commitment to take part, it was simply that with the letters in his possession Cooke could go to potential sponsors in South Africa with proof that a rebel tour by English players was more than just a pipedream.

In the years that have followed the tour many of the participants have said that they were surprised by the three-year ban that was handed down by Lord's under pressure from other cricketing countries and they never envisaged being banned from the Test arena. In my mind those people have been very naïve. From the moment Boycott outlined his plan I realised that a two-, three-, five-year or even life ban from the game was on the cards. Any tour to South Africa which flew in the face of public opinion and government policy was bound to become a hot potato and no one was going to get away with it scot-free.

Although my eyes were wide open to the possible consequences my motives for going were quite simple. In my early twenties with a young wife, I was being given a rare opportunity to set myself up financially. We had been told that anyone going to South Africa would be 'well looked after' and although I never got around to discussing exact figures I expected that to mean at the very least we would be compensated for the loss of earnings that might arise from a period out of the game and a bit more on top.

At the end of that first meeting Boycott urged upon us all the need for secrecy but when, during the following summer, I heard nothing more from him I thought the project had died. I played in the first three Ashes Tests against Australia at home in 1981 and although I later got injured and lost my form I was still picked to go to India with Keith Fletcher's side. In the short period between the end of the domestic season and our departure I heard from Boycott out of the blue. He asked that I attend another meeting, this time at the Holiday Inn in Kensington, along with Gooch and Mike Gatting. Helen came along and sat drinking in the bar with Gatting's wife while we all went upstairs to meet Cooke for the first time.

He turned out to be a tall, dark haired, smooth talking man in his thirties and was accompanied by Stuart Banner, the South African marketing manager for Holiday Inns. Although I didn't know it at the time they had already met with several other players around the country and were planning to see more before the Indian tour got underway. Cooke and Banner outlined between them proposals for a rebel tour that was to take place the following March virtually straight after the end of the official tour to India and Sri Lanka and to impress upon us how serious matters were Banner added that the hotel chain was prepared to put up £500,000, though there was still no discussion on individual salaries. The meeting only served to deepen my interest because while I was back in England's plans for the winter, I had actually ended the season playing in Kent's second eleven and was well aware of how fickle life's fortunes can be towards a fast bowler.

Somehow the timing of all our meetings seemed to coincide with events happening elsewhere. On this occasion it was the Indian government that had decided to mix politics with sport. Word was sifting through from the sub-continent that Mrs Indira Gandhi's ruling party was under pressure to cancel the England tour because anti-apartheid agitators were opposed to the presence of Boycott and Geoff Cook in our squad since both of them had played cricket in South Africa. In fact there were more than two players with such connections, but they had been singled out and for a time it was touch and go whether we would ever set foot in India.

My third and final meeting with the rebels came during the first Test in Bombay a couple of months later when I was introduced by Boycott to another of Cooke's contacts, a South African agent called Peter Venison. Sitting in a room at the Taj Mahal Hotel I learned that Bob Willis had become interested in the tour and that was to have a large bearing on my later decision not to take part. Venison gave us all a lot more details of the four week trip and although some figures of around £50,000 per man were floated about I never did get to learn exactly what the South Africans were prepared to pay for my services.

Before we broke up Venison and Boycott asked all the players to make a final decision on whether to take part in the rebel tour within the next few days. The first to withdraw was Gatting. Although he was still not firmly established in the England team I thought he was concerned about the effects the tour might have on his North London sports shop. David Gower was the next to go explaining that he had little support for South Africa and its politics, but had many friends and business connections in the Caribbean which might be affected if he went.

Their decisions had no bearing on my own since they were both specialist batsmen, I was looking far more closely at the positions of Botham and Willis. At that stage they were both firm favourites to join the rebels and it quickly occurred to me that if a ban was handed down by Lord's, as it surely would be, England would suddenly be left without its two leading strike bowlers. For a young player like myself who had been in and out of the side for almost three years I could see the possibility of becoming a Test regular for years to come and it was an opportunity not to be missed whatever sort of money the South Africans were going to offer.

By the end of the Bombay Test I had informed the others of my decision to pull out but agreed that I would continue to observe the wall of secrecy that still surrounded the whole affair. I felt it was the right thing to do because they had been good enough to take me into their confidence from the start and having gone along with them so far I did not think that it was my job to wreck their tour just because I had decided it did not suit my own aims.

Looking back mine was a disastrous decision and one I was to regret for years. Botham pulled out during the third Test in Bangalore but his mind took some changing. For a whole week he had close discussions with his agent Reg Hayter and solicitor Allan Herd who had flown to India to explain in detail the probable ramifications of the tour for his many existing commercial contracts. At that stage I was not too concerned but it is not hard to imagine how sick I felt when I learned that Willis only decided not to go in the last few hours before the rebels actually boarded their plane at Heathrow.

I hardly paid any notice when after much debate the Test and County Cricket Board banished the rebels for three years, but the combination of Botham and Willis being available to take the new ball for England was to cost me dearly for years to follow. Over the next thirty-six months I played just two one-day internationals and two Tests and I was only picked for the 1983–84 tour to Fiji, New Zealand and Pakistan. In all my income from those few England appearances would barely have reached £17,000. Although the South Africans never talked exact details with me I had known what sort of money I would have wanted. I would have wanted compensation for all the tours and

Tests that I would have been available for during a ban and over three years that would have meant a minimum of £50,000.

I was not the only one to feel fed up after turning down the rebels and I felt deepest sympathy for Keith Fletcher. Having led England in India, but being kept out of the South African conversations to save him from a clash of loyalties with his players, he received a sizeable offer from the rebels shortly after he returned home. He turned it down out of hand because he had high hopes of captaining England against India and Pakistan the following summer. Fletcher, however, lost his job as soon as Peter May took over as chairman of selectors. Despite the loyalty he had shown he was never called upon to play for his country again. In hindsight financially I would have been a lot better off to have gone to South Africa. If there is the possibility of me being invited to go there on another tour I, as a professional cricketer, would be bound to look at it carefully.

Although money had always been my main motive when talking about the tour I had been intrigued about South Africa for some years as my brother-in-law, Graham Johnson, who lived in Johannesburg for several winters, had spent hours talking about the place with Helen and me.

Many of the eventual rebels have refused to talk about the political implications of their tour hiding behind the excuse that as professional cricketers they felt entitled to ply their trade wherever they wished, but I have since been to the country on three separate occasions and it amazes me just how much the whole situation there is misunderstood. Almost daily the British public is fed a diet of thousands of words, either written or spoken on the apartheid issue. But much of it comes from either writers or politicians who have never set foot there and to comprehend fully what is going on, South Africa has to be visited.

In my travels around the dressing rooms of the county cricket circuit I have spoken on many occasions about South Africa and apartheid with players coming from a West Indian background. I know how people like Viv Richards, Wilf Slack and others feel that they have an affinity with the blacks of South Africa and regard them as brothers struggling to break free from a tyrannical regime. But all too often their arguments have simply reduced the issue to a battle between black and white interests, but in my visits there I have found things to be totally different.

I have learned that for centuries black South Africans have been living their own way of life with their own pace of development and they have not had much contact with so called Western standards. I will state categorically that the apartheid system is wrong. It could never be morally acceptable for one set of human beings, viz the white minority, to deny another set the basic human rights of being able to live where they want, vote how they want or marry whom they want.

The problems of apartheid have to be looked at through more understanding eyes. It's all too easy for outsiders to typecast the people of South Africa simply as 'blacks' or 'coloureds' but those labels do not take into account the many different tribes some of whom for centuries have fostered rivalries. I fear that if the white supremacy was to be dismantled at a stroke, as many anti-apartheid factions insist, then those tribes would resort to violence for supremacy and those people who have demanded an instant end to the evils of apartheid would have to accept some share of the blame for whatever happened.

Before anybody accuses me of living the closetted life of a professional cricketer on my three winter trips to South Africa I can assure them that I have seen the type of thing that can go on under the present system. The best illustration I can give is a true tale told me when I was out in Durban in the winter of 1985–86 playing for Glenwood Old Boys and Natal. Among my teammates was Richard Scott the young Hampshire second XI batsman who was sharing a house at the time with two other guys. One day that winter their young black gardener knocked on the door and asked for his lunch. Since Scott was well aware that a meal was part of the boy's wages he duly went into the kitchen and fixed something up. That night, however, Scott was threatened with eviction from his digs when the owner of the house returned to find that the gardener had been fed on one of the plates he used for his own dinner. It is only a small tale of the bigotry that does exist and I have never tried to turn a blind eye to it.

Undoubtedly the hard-headed Afrikaaners, descendants of the original Dutch settlers, would like to see an even tougher system introduced but there are more reasonable politicians slowly emerging who want to see change in the country, but even they accept that it will not be done in one clean sweep and I think it is time that people who advocate boycotting the country accept that fact.

When I was first approached about going on the rebel tour I freely admit that money was my main incentive and I felt that as a professional sportsman I had the right to offer my services to the highest bidder. The moralists would have refused to have acknowledged that and would have denounced me had I gone for appearing to show support for a hated regime, but such reactions I believe are now having a counter effect inside South Africa.

Even some of the moderates inside the Republic are beginning to become tired of what they regard as too much interference from outside in the affairs of their country. The hard liners are beginning to rebel against it and some of the changes that people want to see carried through are now further away than ever. Having sampled that sort of backlash against the various boycotts I am all in favour of a different course of action. To encourage the growing band of reformers I would prefer to see links with South Africa reestablished particularly sporting ones.

The effect it would have could be called 'positive persuasion'. There is very little chance of getting people to change the system if no channels exist through which factions can talk. With cricket, at least, very strong arguments exist for rebuilding bridges since the South African Cricket Union has perhaps done more than any other body in promoting the cause of multi-racial sport. Immediately opponents would cry that there are no blacks playing at first class level but they again conveniently ignore a simple fact of South African life and that is that the blacks are far more interested in soccer than cricket. Furthermore in the winter of 1986–87 the South African selectors actually picked a coloured man, Omar Henry, to face the touring rebel Australians in an unofficial Test match.

Inside South Africa too there is a movement which has for years been deliberately trying to prevent the efforts of the SACU to make the game open to people of all classes and creeds. The opposition has come from the coloured dominated South African Cricket Board and its leader Hassan Howa. He has often been quoted overseas as saying there could be no normal sport in an abnormal society, but put into effect his policies have gone far deeper.

Apart from refusing to allow players affiliated to the board to play alongside whites Howa actively discouraged coloured children from taking part in the coaching courses organised by SACU and using many English professional cricketers who travel to South Africa each winter seeking a job. Many of them could not have given a damn about the colour of the skins of their pupils but Howa was depriving his supporters of the opportunity of improving their skills.

The obstructive efforts of Howa should be compared to some of the achievements of the South African Cricket Union and many clubs not least of all in getting some small parts of apartheid dismantled. In the late seventies they refused to accept government rules that prevented cricketers from two different races drinking together in the same bar at the close of play or the segregation of fans around grounds. With SACU clubs standing defiant the government was forced to alter its laws.

Over the years SACU has made various attempts to get the International Cricket Conference to recognise its achievements but efforts to be readmitted to the Test arena have been constantly blocked. I am convinced that the continued refusal of the ICC to recognise what was actually going on in South African cricket is the main reason why so many rebel tours have been organised to the country.

Faced with total isolation despite its many efforts towards multi racial cricket the officials of SACU finally gave up trying to persuade other nations to help them in their fight for reforms and simply turned to their own devices and I do not blame them for it. Had they been shown more sympathy at a time when the South African government was beginning to bow down to their demands I am sure the rebel tours would not have taken place. With the current status quo there is no discourse at all at official level with the cricket authorities in South Africa and that cannot be a good thing either for the game or for the people – whether they be black, white or coloured – who wish to play it. Sadly the matter seems no longer a cricketing decision but is in the hands of politicians.

5

Remoulding the Style

It was Alan Knott with all his vast experience of ninety-five Test matches for England who inspired me to try and work my way out of the problems that affected my bowling throughout the 1981 Ashes series and the subsequent tour to India and Sri Lanka. I had been unable to find any reasons why I could not bowl at the stumps and at times had considered I might be better off seeking employment in a different profession. Knott, however, suggested that I should add a new weapon to my armoury and develop an outswinger since up to that point I had been relying mainly on pace and nipping the ball back into batsmen.

My lack of cricket in Sri Lanka followed by a month's break from the game after the tour ended was a vital tonic and when Kent went into training before the start of the 1982 season I was ready to face up to the challenge but also felt that everything would have to be handled correctly. At the end of that season, in which I bowled 466 overs for Kent and took 54 wickets, *Wisden* recognised the struggle I went through when it reported 'In the end though the main bowling consolation was provided by Graham Dilley who had dedicated himself, backed by manager Brian Luckhurst, to do things his way throughout the summer.' That simple sentence, however, did not tell the full story.

I did seek out Luckhurst early on and explain what I had in mind but virtually asked to be left alone in the nets to sort things out my own way. During our conversation he agreed but when we got outside into the nets he began to interfere. It was only small things like asking if I wanted any help or offering to stand as an umpire and tell me how I was progressing, but the advances were not welcome. He was probably

Did so much need changing? (*Patrick Eagar*)

60

trying to be seen to be doing enough to justify his position as manager/coach while not being overzealous so that he would have to carry the can if my bowling went totally to pot because of the experiment. Whatever his motives they got my back up and several of our pre-season nets ended in us both having a stand-up row in public. In the end, since my contract was due to expire the following September, I decided to go totally my own way and it was going to be up to the county to decide later whether they still wished to retain my services.

The outswinger was taking good shape midway through May when the selectors called me up to Lord's for the MCC match against the Indians and I was not too displeased to take 5 for 69, especially after the weeks of frustration on the dead wickets of the sub-continent the previous winter. The victims were impressive too as I removed Pronob Roy, Ghulam Parkar and Dilip Vengsarkar who were the first three in the Indian order, before cleaning up the tail by knocking over Suru Nayak and Shivlal Yadav. With the selectors clearly impressed I was included in the squads for the one-day international and even played in the opening game at the Oval where seven overs cost me just nineteen runs, but that was the last time England turned to me that summer.

In many ways it was not a bad thing that the selectors looked at the likes of Derek Pringle, Ian Greig and Norman Cowans because with my new method of bowling still very much going through a learning stage it would not have been right to be seen experimenting in the high pressure atmosphere of Test cricket. Keeping me going was the thought that I was still only twenty-two years old and young enough to have a long future ahead of me with England once everything had been sorted out.

The side for that following winter's tour was chosen while Kent were involved in a championship match with Leicestershire at Canterbury and since David Gower was due to be vice-captain in Australia and New Zealand I had a quiet word with him after hearing that he had received a lunch time phone call from Bob Willis. He simply said 'sorry, no' when I asked if I was in the squad, though I felt far better equipped at the time to play for England than I had been twelve months earlier when Keith Fletcher nominated me for India. I proved the point by taking ten Leicestershire wickets in the match, which at the time was my best return for the county.

The thought that I might need employment that winter had occurred to me weeks earlier and with help from Graham Johnson and his contacts in South Africa I had already made arrangements to play for the Wanderers Club in Johannesburg, though there was a clause in my contract saying it could be cancelled if England wanted me.

The Wanderers sent a deputation to meet Helen and me at the airport and since we had been on the same flight as Johnson and Alvin Kallicharran there was a sizeable number of officials waiting when we arrived. Among them was the former South African Test batsman Ali Bacher and having heard so much about him from Johnson it was arranged that we should be introduced but I was not expecting the greeting I received. He refused to shake my hand and said with a certain amount of spite 'You will never ever play for Transvaal' and turned away. Playing for the state that winter was hardly on my mind but in the days that followed it occurred to me that Bacher may have been bearing a grudge following my decision to pull out of the rebel tour the previous spring.

My welcome at the Wanderers was quite the opposite. Whilst in my teens I had played club cricket in England and I could not believe the organisation I had joined for the winter. Because of the structure of cricket in South Africa where the best players still turn out for their clubs when they are not involved in state games, the standard was much higher than I had been expecting. It was not unusual to play a club match against opposition which might have as many as three or four capped Springboks in their ranks. As I was still attempting to remould my bowling it was gratifying to be able to face top-class batsmen.

Behind the scenes the officials at the Wanderers were also extremely helpful. When Helen and I first arrived we were put up in a small flat that had been fine for its previous bachelor resident, Peter Stringer the Yorkshire player, but hardly big enough for the two of us. We did not like to make a complaint but once the Wanderers' secretary heard about our discomfort he said he would be happy if we could find ourselves somewhere else to live. After a week of flat hunting Helen and I finally found somewhere suitable and to my surprise there was absolutely no opposition from the club even though they were forced to fork out twice the amount of rent. Knowing what Kent's reaction might have been in a similar situation I was staggered when I worked out, with air fares and my small living expenses, what the Wanderers were prepared to pay for my services that winter.

There were other bonuses too since the Wanderers is far more than just a cricket club. If I wanted to swim there was an Olympic-sized pool

63

available and for keen divers another pool with Olympic-standard boards. For rackets enthusiasts the club had around twenty squash courts and fifty more for tennis and since I was still interested in golf I was not averse to making use of the Wanderers' championship standard course. Their main cricket ground, where South Africa had staged many famous Tests was leased out to the Transvaal Cricket Union, but the pitch we played on elsewhere in the complex was comparable to the best back in England.

In such a brilliant setting I settled down for an enjoyable winter but around Christmas there was one awkward incident. Since there had been no suggestion that I might make the Transvaal side Helen and I had arranged with friends to go to the coast south of Durban for a Christmas break which coincided with a Currie Cup game between Transvaal and Natal. Transvaal, however, were suffering from an injury crisis with their three main strike bowlers – Vince Van Der Bijl, Neal Radford and Spook Hanley – and none of them was available to play. I knew that I was qualified to step in but judging by Bacher's comments at the airport three months earlier I was certain I would not be picked. Bacher, however summoned me to his office early one morning and said he was considering me and would I like to play for Transvaal. While I said yes in theory I was not prepared to let down the friends with whom I had arranged the holiday, despite Bacher's offer to fly me back to Johannesberg specifically for the match. I insisted I would not go back on my word to friends, which was a subtle way of suggesting to Bacher that he was not sticking to his own earlier comments. In the end I went away and there was no further invitation to play for Transvaal during my stay.

The rest of the winter passed all too quickly as we made plenty of friends in Johannesberg, I threw myself into my club cricket with the Wanderers and rebuilt confidence in my bowling. And the benefit of the visit quickly showed when the 1983 championship season began again with Kent. Our early programme included a potentially tough fixture against Essex at Chelmsford and my first ball uprooted Graham Gooch's stumps. I went on to take 5 for 70 in twenty-one pretty hostile overs and although the second day was washed out by rain, after each side had forfeited an innings we achieved a notable six wicket victory.

Although May served up its traditional bout of wet weather I also took wickets in our other two championship matches against Surrey and Hampshire which impressed the selectors sufficiently for me to be included in their squad for the third World Cup. I took four wickets in

Warren Lees can only admire the power as I make contact during the 1983 World Cup. (*Patrick Eagar*)

our second qualifying match against Sri Lanka but it was when we met Pakistan in the following game at Lord's that I felt I was back at my best. I ended their innings wicketless but conceded just 33 runs from my twelve overs and more importantly bowled as fast and as accurately as I had ever done before and it was all a tremendous relief.

Such is fate, however, that the effects of playing seven high pressured one-day internationals in such a short space of time took a heavy toll on me. By the time the first Test of the summer against New Zealand was played at the Oval I was injured suffering stress-related shin problems. I was back in time for the second Test at Leeds where the Kiwis recorded their first ever victory on English soil by five wickets but I failed to get among the visitors' batting, despite much playing and missing, and was not included for the final two Tests of the series at Lord's and Trent Bridge.

A series of niggling injuries also restricted my appearances for Kent as the county made substantial progress in the NatWest Trophy. I missed the quarter-final victory over Warwickshire at Canterbury and was frustrated to sit out the semi-final with Hampshire, but fortunately recovered in time to make an appearance at Lord's against Somerset. It was an important match for all the Kent players who had continually had to put up with comparisons to the highly successful squad which won eight trophies in the seventies.

Although we managed to limit Somerset to 193 for 9 from their fifty overs our batsmen never quite mastered the big West Indian Joel Garner who bowled nine overs for just 15 runs nor Vic Marks who took 3 for 30, and we lost by 24 runs. Our dressing room was like a morgue afterwards having gone so close to silencing our many critics within the county – we knew they would soon forget that we had managed to reach a final and they were only interested in trophies not runners up.

Although I bitterly hated losing there was some consolation in store for me since the selectors had taken notice of my personal performance. In ten overs that cost only 29 runs and, helped by cloud overhead and moisture in the pitch, I got the wickets of Peter Denning, Peter Roebuck, Viv Richards and Nigel Popplewell. The big match atmosphere generated by a crowd of twenty-three thousand had brought the best out of me and England acknowledged it with a place on the winter tour to New Zealand and Pakistan.

RIGHT: Another vital wicket as Viv Richards departs in the 1983 NatWest Trophy Final at Lord's.

OPPOSITE: 'That's the one we wanted' – sheer delight as I remove Pakistan dangerman Zaheer Abbas at Old Trafford during the 1983 World Cup.

6

A Winter of Frustration

In the years before the widespread introduction of passenger jet airliners when all overseas tours began with a leisurely sea voyage on board ship it was not unusual for England players to wave goodbye to their wives and loved ones at the end of one county championship season and only return home the following spring just in time for the start of the next. More recently, however, the planning of winter tours has changed pretty dramatically.

With hotel costs and air fares continually on the increase and players rather less willing to spend so much time away from their families the tour planners at the Test and County Cricket Board have been forced to try to fit a quart into a pint pot. Their attempts have been further hampered by the seemingly insatiable appetite in some countries for a growing number of one-day international fixtures. The net result is that on most international tours there have been far fewer rest days and a cutback in the number of warm-up matches played.

That was certainly the case on the 1983–84 trip to Fiji, New Zealand and Pakistan where I was to spend day after frustrating day sitting on the sidelines or working in the nets. I was unable to break into the England team because with no practice matches after the first month of the tour I had no opportunity to prove to the selectors that I was in good enough form to challenge for a place. And after embarking on a tour with such high hopes and expectations I eventually went home early with a serious injury which threatened to end my cricketing career at the tender age of twenty-four.

When we took off from Gatwick shortly after Christmas I was far fitter than I had been at the start of my three previous tours. Losing the previous summer's NatWest Bank Trophy final at Lord's to Somerset by 24 runs had shaken me up badly. But in the months that followed before the tour got underway I managed to turn my disappointment into a new driving will to win and to bring about a change of fortune I realised I had to get myself in proper shape. Consequently in the weeks leading up to the tour I ran a minimum of four miles every day finishing off the week with the equivalent of a half marathon every Friday.

Even so my new found reserves of stamina were to be pushed to the limit as we opened the tour with two one-day games against Fiji. It was not so much the heat and high humidity – it was over ninety degrees in the shade during our first game at Nandi – but the tremendous hospitality showered on us by the Islanders. No English side had visited Fiji since Douglas Jardine's bodyline merchants had stopped off there on their way from the 1933 tour to Australia and the locals were determined that it was not going to be another fifty years before England returned. Even though it was gone four o'clock in the morning when we arrived from London, via San Francisco, we were greeted with a champagne reception complete with a local folk band and on New Year's Eve our hotel laid on a special dinner combined with a display of local folk dancing.

Part of the programme called for us all to be introduced to the delights of Yaqona – an uninviting muddy-coloured concoction made from soaking the roots of the pepper plant. We were told that at the time scientists in America were studying the potion since the locals claimed it had marvellous powers for curing stomach disorders. Although I took one sip and decided that was enough one journalist who drank seven bowls full swore by the end of the evening that it would make a fairly effective anaesthetic.

With Mike Gatting going on a six-hitting spree while scoring 142 we gave the Fijians a good demonstration in our opening game piling up 274 for 6 from our fifty overs and then bowling them out for just 76. I got two early wickets and, conceding just eleven runs in seven overs, was fairly satisfied. Forty-eight hours later, however, we all nearly had egg on our face as the Fijians went close to winning the return played on the other side of the Island in the capital Suva. On a matting wicket of dubious quality we only managed to score 146 and they got within 18 runs of our total. The tension at the end of the second game aroused the local fans and it would be nice to think that on future tours England could stop off at some other small cricketing outposts and spread the gospel of the game. I know excursions to places like Singapore and Hong Kong would be enthusiastically received.

Fortunately the climate in New Zealand was not quite so harsh as we set out to play three warm-up matches before the first Test at Wellington and it soon became obvious that I would be competing for the fourth seam bowler's spot in the side with Norman Cowans.

Neil Foster had already clinched the third fast bowling place alongside Bob Willis and Ian Botham with an impressive six wicket performance against Northern Districts at Hamilton, but I felt pretty sick when I learned at the pre-test team meeting that Cowans had been voted in ahead of me. The decision hurt all that much more after all the extra effort I had been putting in during our training sessions and as the team broke up I deliberately stayed behind to find out the reason from Willis. I felt that there was very little point in keeping quiet when I thought I should have been playing. But when, having explained my views on the choice, he said that Cowans had been bowling better the previous summer I got even more angry.

For a start there had been five months between the end of the English season and the first Test and there was no guarantee that Cowans had retained his form. I did not think it went back to the previous summer because a week earlier during our game against Central Districts at Palmerston North I had known that Willis and our assistant manager Norman Gifford had made a special effort to compare the form of both Cowans and myself. They kept walking from end to end at the ground to study both of our actions from behind the arm and we had even commented on it between overs. In fact the two of us bowled about the same pace and although Cowans got three wickets to my one during the game I conceded only one and a half runs an over compared to Cowans who went for nearly three so there was not that much to choose between us.

Historically in such circumstances English selectors both at home and abroad have tended to opt for the bowler with the better record as a batsman in which case there should not have been any difficulty in coming to a decision. From my earliest schooldays I had been considered something of a batsman and at Under-13 and Under-14 level I was in fact batting in the top six for Kent schoolboys and only bowling occasionally. Over the years as my bowling developed I paid less attention to scoring runs and lacked the talent to score heavily at first-class level, but I already had two Test fifties under my belt by that stage of my career and when it came to a comparison with Cowans about batting there was none to be made.

I wondered how the selectors had managed to forget that I had taken part in that famous 117 run stand with Botham at Headingley in 1981 and the following winter had actually been chosen for two Tests specifically to fill a spot in the middle order batting at seven. Knowing that Cowans' record could not touch mine it made Willis' limp excuse even worse and I was even more unhappy by the time our little chat came to an end. I went back to my hotel room and kicked the bed a couple of times out of sheer frustration.

In the event England drew the first Test when at one stage we might have won it while Cowans was finally made twelfth man. Botham took five wickets as the Kiwis were shot out for 219 and then featured in an exciting 232 run partnership with Derek Randall which earned us a substantial 244 run first innings lead. Unfortunately the Wellington wicket got slow and flatter as the match went on and New Zealand, led by centuries from Jeremy Coney and Martin Crowe, easily escaped with a draw.

But since we had once been in a winning position I knew that if I was to make the Test team for the second game at Christchurch I had to put on an impressive performance when we travelled south to meet Otago in Dunedin. The fates however, had obviously decided to gang up against me because, after taking three wickets, I pulled up with a thigh strain that was to keep me out of the reckoning for the next month, though it need not have been so long.

Initially I went to see our long standing physio Bernie Thomas, but with my limited knowledge of physiotherapy I was frustrated by the time it was taking to get me fit. On his tours overseas Thomas was always one for new gadgets and that winter he had acquired a small electronic pulse machine which all the lads nicknamed Radio Turkey. I was told that basically it deadened the nerve ends around an injured area and while I felt the thigh was actually getting better because I could feel no pain at all in fact it had not changed and what I thought should have been corrected in four days of treatment was still causing me difficulties ten days later.

By the time I had returned to full fitness the second Test had been played and lost by an innings in under three days at Christchurch – we were twice bowled out on a minefield of a pitch for 82 and 93 – and with there being no more practice matches in the itinerary for the tour my chances of pressing a claim for a Test recall were slim. Ironically had the thigh cleared up quickly I would have played in the Christchurch disaster because Foster was suffering from a broken toe after being struck in the nets by Willis who also had an injury problem. With me out of the running the selectors in desperation called up Sussex's Tony Pigott who had chosen to spend his winter playing club cricket in New Zealand and had been due to marry on the fifth day of the Test.

71

Waiting for a return during the one-day international at Lahore in 1984. (*Adrian Murrell*)

OPPOSITE: Another fruitless appeal for lbw against Mudassar Nazar. (*Adrian Murrell*)

Ironically since the game ended inside three days Pigott could have made it to the altar, but by then he had postponed his plans and it was to be some months before the knot was sealed.

Seeing Pigott take what I thought should be my rightful place in the side and with the thigh still playing up I knew that the strain needed treatment from an ultrasound machine and although Thomas did not have one with him I discovered a local physio in a Christchurch hotel gym who was more than happy to have me as a patient. Determined to be fit I got permission from the management to use this outside help and as I expected the ultrasound quickly had me back on my feet again and raring to go.

73

ABOVE: Pakistan can be a frustrating place and at Faisalabad I actually beat the
pitch as Salim Malik is caught behind off a no ball. (*Adrian Murrell*)
OPPOSITE: You've got to be joking: Graeme Fowler pressed into service as an
emergency wicket-keeper against Pakistan at Lahore. (*Adrian Murrell*)

Because so few people knew about that extra treatment and the
lengths I was prepared to go to get it I was very upset a month later in
Pakistan when I was finally called up to play in the second Test at
Faisalabad. In the *Guardian* Matthew Engel wrote that the selectors
would have liked to have picked me much earlier on the tour but were
unable to get the message through the headphones of my portable
stereo. Apart from being a slur on my professionalism as a cricketer (for
which at one stage I seriously considered demanding an apology) it
was also completely untrue.

From my earliest days in the game I had learned to try to ignore what

75

Soft drinks only in Pakistan. (*Adrian Murrell*)

had been written about me in the papers. While praise had always helped boost my ego and confidence, criticism had never really been needed since inside myself I always knew whether or not I had a bad day in the field. But I could not expect people like my parents to take the same attitude and from thousands of miles away I was in no position to try to correct an impression which was clearly wrong.

I had demonstrated to my captain at least how keen I was to get a slice of the action, but since it was shrouded in secrecy people back in England, of course, were not to know the real position, but I still wonder to this day how many *Guardian* readers were influenced by his rather cheap and tasteless attempt to be witty at my expense. That one sentence certainly hurt me more than any of the other thousands of words that had been written about my career.

Still I think my attitude managed to impress Willis. He said at the end of the tour that I had been given a fairly good report and I would like to think that was because from the outset I had queried my omission from the team and then taken active steps to get myself included.

During the six weeks in which I played no competitive cricket at all my moods did change, however. It is a fact of life that in every tour party there are one or two players, nicknamed 'Lord Lucans' who are only on the verge of the Test side who find themselves unemployed for long stretches at a time. For cricketers used to playing non-stop week in and week out for their counties it is a new and strange experience.

The spare batsmen on tour have always tended to suffer more than the bowlers because by nature the latter breed suffer more from injuries and the whims of the selectors at the slightest loss of form. Nevertheless I had never found myself in that position on my previous three tours and I found it difficult to adjust. I had embarked on the tour full of determination, but with no chance of proving the selectors wrong I began to fret. That did not seem to help and despite all my early intentions I found myself throwing in the towel, accepting that I was destined not to get a game and just eagerly looking forward to the flight home and hoping that a new English season would bring with it a change of luck.

But it was around the end of our time in New Zealand that a new problem arose that was to have a dramatic effect on my life. One night after yet another frustrating day in the nets I ran myself a hot bath but when I put my right leg in the water it only felt tepid. Naturally enough I added even more hot water and when the bath still did not feel hot to my right leg I just accepted that the hotel must have been having problems with its boiler. I resigned myself to having a bath in cold water and got the shock of my life when I stuck my left leg in only to discover that the water was in fact scalding hot and I realised that I had no feeling whatsoever in my right leg.

At the time I was still too desperate to get back into the England side to report the problem to the tour management. It had not stopped me training and when I was finally needed by the team in Faisalabad I felt quite capable of doing a proper job. In any event we were running short of players since Willis had been forced to hand over the reigns to David Gower. Our captain was confined to his bed in an old style colonial club where we were billeted, suffering from a severe bout of stomach trouble – what was surprising was that more of his colleagues had not gone down with the same problem. We were being expected to perform at our best for six hours a day in extreme heat without a decent hotel to return to in the evenings and forced to eat food that after being transported for three hours by road from Lahore was not at its best. With Botham struggling to overcome a knee condition that was to require an operation before the month of March was out England needed me to play and I was determined to take my first chance of the winter.

Bowling in a match however, produced a strange sensation. While I could run normally I could not feel my right foot landing at the crease and I wasn't helped by a lack of rhythm after such a long lay off that caused me to bowl six no-balls in the my first over. Overstepping in that match actually led to stories that Gower had been forced to have a strong word in my ear when it appeared that I had displayed public dissent at the standard of the two Pakistani umpires, but again it was far from the truth. The incident arose as Salim Malik was building a cultured 116 in Pakistan's first innings. Bowling from one end I managed to shatter his stumps but was called for a no-ball. Later, having switched ends, I had the same batsman caught behind only to be pulled up for overstepping again. In sheer frustration I sank to my knees and beat the ground with my fists but it had nothing at all to do with the umpire.

I was merely exasperated that having got the batsman out on the flattest of wickets I had twice been denied by the lack of a constant run-up caused by my spell of inactivity. Gower knew how I felt and although from the press box eighty yards away it may have looked as though I was getting a ticking off in fact he was just encouraging me.

Still, with no help from the pitch, and I would have hated to have to try to bowl on that track every week, I managed to return figures of 3 for 101 in 28 overs. Proof of just how much of a batting paradise had been prepared, showed in the final scorecard after Pakistan won the first Test in Karachi. Of the bowlers in that Test on either side only Sarfraz Nawaz and myself managed to take more than two wickets in the whole five days. We easily came out with a draw after Gower scored 152 to offer the selectors ample evidence that if he were to be handed the captaincy at some later date on a more permanent basis his form with the bat would not suffer.

While I was worrying about my dead leg, and the numbness was gradually creeping up my right side, another storm was brewing on the tour. Whispers began to reach us from London that the *Mail on Sunday* had launched a major investigation into rumours that Ian Botham had been smoking marijuana during our stay in New Zealand and had dispatched two reporters to Lahore to interview players and the management team. I don't know to this day whether there was any substance to the allegations, but it made a rough tour even tougher. I had to feel sorry for our manager Alan 'AC' Smith. Popular with the players, Smith had been through a torrid time on his first tour to the West Indies and now he found himself in another red hot situation. Although Geoff Boycott once said Smith tried to extract the maximum amount of drama out of any given situation, I always felt he handled things pretty well even though decisions sometimes took a long time in coming.

The thought of England players taking drugs was bound to stir up controversy. Personally I did not smoke marijuana though I had strong views on the issue which coincided with the often quoted thoughts of ex-Beatle Paul McCartney. He felt that there was nothing wrong in an individual taking a soft non-addictive drug providing the user is not selling them on the streets or attempting to influence other people, specifically youngsters. I totally disagree with hard drug taking and any link between sport and drugs.

What I could not accept at the time was the way the two newspapermen went about their job. They spent most of their days hanging around the lobby of the Hilton Hotel in Lahore, buttonholing anyone who went past and it turned the whole team into a bunch of recluses. We could not leave our rooms without being approached and they even grabbed Cowans in a lift and tried to get him to sign some sort of statement.

It was a difficult time too for the genuine cricket writers who had been with us since we had left England and as in most cases they had travelled on a number of previous overseas tours, they were regarded as colleagues and in some instances even close friends. They only wanted to write about the cricket and with Willis ill, Botham about to go home for a cartilage operation and a Test series being played there was plenty enough of that. But once the *Mail on Sunday* went ahead and published its allegations, despite our management's strenuous denials, they were forced to become involved. Their loyalties were obviously divided and I could not understand how editors back in London were expecting their cricket writers to pick up all the on-the-field stories from players at the same time as being expected to crucify them off it. Over the ten years I had been involved in the game it had become increasingly apparent that some papers were no longer interested in the game of cricket itself but more with searching for scandal. The drugs story was to be the start of a long and sustained campaign against the English team and Botham in particular and the whole trend deeply upset players and genuine lovers of cricket.

By the end of the tour we were accused, particularly by the influential *Cricketer* magazine, of lacking pride in playing for England and discipline. It was an easy attack to level at us since we lost Test series in New Zealand and Pakistan for the first time, but it was a flawed argument. At the start of that tour, as on any other tour, the players were keen to succeed but the days had long since gone when any Test series could be seen as a pushover. The overall standard in Test cricket had risen as countries played more against each other and England had no divine right to success.

Our critics however would not accept that. They turned a blind eye to the fact that we simply had not performed well or had been outplayed by the opposition and instead chose to find reasons for our defeats, sometimes made up, off the field of play. Three years later when I travelled to Australia and helped England win three trophies there was no more determination or better behaviour from the players than there had been on that trip to New Zealand and Pakistan, but the winning sides face few problems compared to those that lose. It is a standard excuse that a losing side has lost pride in itself but in all the years I had been involved in England teams I had yet to come across one player who said he could not give a damn while playing for his country.

While all the furore about drugs was breaking around us I decided that the time had come to report my leg condition to Thomas who immediately called in a Pakistani doctor. After first talking over the problem he later confirmed the extent of the numbness by sticking a pin in various parts of my anatomy. The lack of feeling had reached up to just below my ribs and something clearly had to be done, but I was wary when he suggested that I undergo some tests.

With all due respect to the Pakistani Health Service I did not fancy being admitted to a local hospital after hearing some harrowing stories about the conditions I might find. Offered the choice by Thomas, I opted to catch the next flight to London. It had been a long and disappointing tour for me personally and I could not wait to get back to Helen.

Although there was still a Test to be played England lost the services of Dilley, Botham and Willis within the space of a week. I was to be out of Test action for two years, Botham had a cartilage whipped out and was ready for the start of the new season, but Willis lost the England captaincy as a result of a tour that was seen by everyone as a disaster. Although I had nothing personally against Willis he would not have been my choice when he was appointed by Peter May two years earlier. In my view it is difficult for a bowler to be captain and I think he would probably agree, though once offered the job and with a couple of years' experience leading Warwickshire he could hardly have turned it down.

The problem with a bowler who is a captain is that he simply does not have enough time on the field to concentrate properly on two jobs. When he was wound up trying to sort out his problems as a captain Willis probably did not give enough time to his bowling and vice versa and since his career was nearing its end he probably needed more time mentally on his bowling than anything else. He was often accused of letting Botham bowl too much particularly at Richard Hadlee when his 99 proved so decisive on a bad wicket during the Christchurch Test. But I believe Willis had such faith in Botham that he was happy to leave him at one end for long periods so that he would only have to concentrate as captain on getting things right at the other end.

Willis had his problems off the field as well since he never was the greatest of communicators. One day he might walk up and have a chat, but the next he could stride straight past you, staring ahead into space and not even saying hello – I had got used to that since playing with him in my early days but it was hardly the ideal way for the captain of a team to behave. All that said I am sure Willis did his best to cope with

81

the leadership but I was not surprised to see Gower given the job full time when England returned home for the summer series against the West Indies.

My own flight back was full of worries about my condition. Although I knew very little about the disease I kept thinking that I had contracted multiple sclerosis. In the week that followed my arrival home I underwent test after test to discover the cause of the numbness and all the time there was a growing fear that I might never play cricket again.

7

The Long Road Back

With the drugs controversy still raging in Pakistan there was a pack of reporters waiting to meet my plane when it landed at Heathrow, but so too were Helen and Donald Carr, the secretary of the Test and County Cricket Board. Although my mystery injury might have been an excuse to give a press conference he was not too happy at the thought of an England player being exposed to the press when other subjects might have arisen and, quite rightly and to my relief, I was not allowed to say a word.

I had barely had time to recover from the flight or even talk to Helen in depth when, within twenty-four hours of arriving home, Kent had made an appointment for me to see club doctor Reg Jones, in Folkestone. Although his initial tests again failed to find the cause of my numbness I was left with the distinct impression that I had something far more seriously wrong with me than just a trapped nerve that could be massaged away under anaesthetic. That had been ruled out because there was no pain whatsoever.

From Folkestone I was referred to Ashford Hospital for more tests under the supervision of a specialist. While he too failed to find the cause I was given a cautionary warning before I left the hospital that I could have contracted an obscure form of cancer or as I feared multiple sclerosis, but even at that stage my concern was not that great. While my parents and Helen began to get pretty worried I was still hoping that it was just another niggling injury and that, like others earlier in my career, it would go away with the passage of time. Perhaps I should have been more worried myself but I was determined not to let morose thoughts of what might be wrong with me creep in until the doctors knew for sure.

With the tests at Ashford again proving blank it was arranged for me to be admitted to Guy's Hospital in London where I was given the full works though some might say the brain scan was a bit of a waste of time. I had given so many blood samples that I was beginning to feel like a pin cushion, but it was the number of holes in my left arm that made a nurse switch over to my right arm and, quite by accident, discover the root of the problem.

She noticed that my right bicep had begun to wither and immediately called in a doctor for a consultation. They decided that a dye should be injected into my spinal column and after allowing it to circulate throughout the system they discovered under x-ray that there was a blockage in my spinal cord around the fifth and sixth vertebrae in my neck.

Because of the danger of the dye getting into the brain and leaving me with a headache as it had done to other patients previously I was kept in hospital while the x-rays were studied and the problem diagnosed. I was told that a disc was actually trapped against the spinal cord, but that an operation involving the removal of the disc and replacing it with a piece of reshaped bone from my left hip could cure the problem. Although I was warned that it would be a delicate process because of the danger of damaging the spinal cord the doctors were pretty confident of success. But there was a cautionary note – if the operation failed it could not be carried out a second time and there was a real danger that I could end up a cripple. There was also no guarantee that the feeling would return.

I must have been pretty relaxed about the whole affair because even the weak pre-med injection knocked me straight out and the next thing I knew I was waking up in the private room laid on for me by the Test and County Cricket Board and feeling slightly uncomfortable. The cause of that was easily explained because the surgeons had actually bolted my head into a certain position to make sure there was no movement which might upset the bone graft but after a couple of days the bolts in my temples were removed and as the long process of recovery began a surgical collar was placed around my neck.

As a precaution against complications that might be caused by an infection to my hip or neck I was kept in hospital for ten days but since I was not actually physically ill I had far more freedom than some of the other patients. I was even allowed to go for a Sunday lunchtime drink with Helen but that led to a security scare. After a couple of pints I slipped back into the hospital without notifying the ward sister who, after several hours, began to panic. Without checking my room she sent out search parties to all the local pubs asking if they had recently seen an England fast bowler.

Life in hospital was made more comfortable by the fact that my operation coincided with the 1984 World Snooker Championships on TV and while I could not turn my head from side to side there was no harm in staring straight ahead at the box which featured the action from Sheffield almost from the end of *Breakfast Time* through to late in the evening. Daily the doctors expressed satisfaction with my progress but there could have been a crisis when Helen finally arrived to take me home.

With my recovery still very much in its infancy it was vital not to subject my neck to any sudden movements, but on the way back to Canterbury I felt pain every time the motion of the car altered as Helen changed gear and it would have only taken an idiot to have driven into the back of our car for me to suffer whiplash injuries and leave the whole operation in ruins.

Throughout that fortnight no one ever mentioned the subject of playing cricket in front of me – they didn't want to build up my hopes or crush them, but there was one clear message coming through. I was left in no doubt that the neck would take several months to heal and that I would be putting myself in grave danger of being paralysed for life if I took any liberties. Utterly convinced I settled down to do absolutely nothing for the summer. People have often asked whether the weeks which turned into months were periods of total boredom but I had always been a lazy creature with dreams of having enough money to sit around all day and do as I please, and while I hadn't got the money I had no choice about being idle. Since I had to sleep in a certain position, which was not totally comfortable, I would wake early each day and move into the lounge to watch TV from the moment *Breakfast Time* started through to the small white dot appearing on the screen at night.

Although Helen must have been frustrated, it never showed, though she did have a part-time job at a chemists and a young horse to school which got her out of the house during the week. At first my only excursions were by foot since I still feared the possibility of being in a car crash and generally I only ever went as far as the nearest pub. As my strength grew, however, two new interests arose. Since Helen had become pregnant with our first child we decided to move to a bigger house and spent several days down in the Canterbury area hunting for our future home and on Sundays I took to the airwaves.

A friend advised me that while I was in the background through injury it would not be a bad thing to try and keep my name in the news.

Nationally that was achieved by several newspaper articles given exclusively to the *Sun*, but locally in Kent I joined the Radio Medway commentary team for the county's Sunday League matches.

The thought of sitting behind a microphone held no fears for me since the tour to India and Sri Lanka in 1982 when I found myself for one afternoon being part of the BBC's commentary team. We were in Jullundur for a one-day international against India when commentator Don Mosey found himself without anyone to share his duties throughout four and a half hours on the air. Paul Allott and I, neither of us being in the side, volunteered to help out between overs – it was a good excuse for passing free messages to the folks back home – and I spent three hours in the box gaining what was to prove valuable experience.

Those Sunday afternoons in 1984 sharing the commentaries with Medway's Steve Brinckley were full of fun and enjoyment though I occasionally found myself being ribbed by my Kent colleagues since Graham Johnson insisted on listening to the broadcasts in the dressing room. Sometimes, however, I fell into the trap which catches many former cricketers when they go on radio and TV and that is referring to my own playing days and criticising what I saw as changes. It is a commentator's habit that infuriates many current cricketers and yet there I was committing the same crime, but it was all too easy to do.

Over the months my visits back to hospital for check-ups grew more and more infrequent and with the doctors satisfied with my progress I began to exercise more as the summer drew to an end. I was even allowed to venture out onto the golf course though the Graham Dilley version of the game bore little resemblance to the textbooks as I could not keep my head still and turn my torso for fear of damaging my neck. I was limited to a short backswing and follow through but at least I was beginning to get out a bit more.

As the restrictions on me eased I began to think of cricket again and after long hours of discussion Helen and I decided that a visit to South Africa sometime in the New Year of 1985 would give me the chance to ease my way back into the game at club level with the outside possibility of reporting back to Kent for pre-season training in April. The doctors did not object and I hoped Kent would help with the air fares to Johannesburg.

Although I thought it would be a good investment on the county's part since the trip represented my best chance of returning to the Kent side that summer, the committee consistently refused my plea for help.

The Johannesburg club side Florida had offered us cheap accommodation and a small fee for playing at weekends, but I had no way of getting out there after a summer of pretty tough financial struggles trying to live off my basic salary without income from Tests. In the end Graham Johnson persuaded a friend of his at Barclays that the bank should come up with the tickets in return for some promotional work and I was duly grateful.

Money was certainly tight at the time. Since no county employs its players during the winter months I was forced throughout the autumn to go on the dole. It was not an idea that appealed to me at first but as our bank balance dwindled I had no choice, despite my pride. In the end I was quite surprised when I went to the Canterbury Social Security to sign on as the local officials were exceedingly helpful, there were very few people around at the time, and after one visit I simply received a cheque through the post every fortnight.

Once I arrived in South Africa officials at the Florida Club went out of their way to help. At first there was no question of me being able to bowl and I spent six weeks in the club side as a batsman. It was in the nets in midweek that I began to turn my arm over, though at first I was only running in off a couple of paces but as the time span since the operation increased I became more adventurous until eventually I was able to bowl in matches as well. When we left South Africa to return home it was virtually a year after the surgeons had operated on my spine and I was once again ready to try first-class cricket.

8

The Winds of Change

The 1986 County Championship season was barely over and the winter tour to Australia had yet to begin when rumours that I was unhappy at Kent and possibly thinking of finding a new employer began to emerge in the press. They were fuelled by the county revealing that I had refused to sign a new two-year contract, which in fact had been on the table for nearly twelve months. But the news was hardly earth shattering since a year earlier I had asked Kent to release me and they had turned me down flat.

It was to be another five months before I received an offer from Mike Jones, the chairman of Worcestershire's cricket committee, which I simply could not turn down. But if any Kent supporters think it was purely a large cash incentive that made me decide my future would be best spent elsewhere, then they are wrong and the time has come to put the record straight once and for all.

The seeds of my discontent had been sown several years previously but it was to take time for a lot of small incidents to grow into a major grouse. Having been born and raised in Dartford and played for the county since the age of seventeen when I made my second eleven debut I had always been a Kent man through and through. The final decision to leave was the toughest I have ever had to make in my life and only time will tell whether I did the right thing. But blind loyalty to Kent could not paper over the cracks which had begun to appear after my first tour with England to Australia in 1979–80.

As I explained earlier in this book, I returned from there as a twenty-year-old with two Test match appearances under my belt and obviously a bright future ahead of me. Kent and I disagreed over money at the end of that trip and it was to be a contentious issue that raised its head a number of times in the ensuing years.

But there had been other fundamental issues as well, not least of all was the type of wickets in the county on which I was expected to

A final attempt to win honours with Kent as I bowl Wilf Slack at Lord's in the
Benson and Hedges Cup final. (*Patrick Eagar*)

perform over the years. Let's face it, some counties in England inevitably prepare their pitches to suit the strengths of their bowling attack and Kent was no exception, but the problem was that successive captains and the cricket committee insisted that our main strike weapon was Derek Underwood so, as far as the seamers were concerned, flat and hopefully turning surfaces were the general requirement. Now I have no personal beef with Derek and cannot help but admire a player who has managed to stay at the top for well over two decades, taking 297 wickets in 86 Tests for England – the other three victims to take him to 300 would surely have gone his way had he not decided to join the 1982 rebel tour to South Africa.

But while Kent were pandering to Underwood's needs it was at the expense of their pace bowlers, including myself. The county expected a lot, but were never prepared to provide the right tools. They wanted me to get the 60, 70 or 80, wickets a year that other people were getting on home grounds that were green, hard seamers. At my pace I need to be able to extract bounce and movement from wickets but it was never there to be had in Kent. Although I cannot talk for the other bowlers in the side, I am sure some felt occasionally that they were banging their heads against brick walls. Certainly in my last season at Kent the policy was sheer folly. While Derek may have been the doyen, the county had assembled a pretty respectable pace attack which, given the right help, could have been far more successful. Both Richard Ellison and I had played for England, we had Australia's Terry Alderman and although Kevin Jarvis had never played for his country, he had twice in the past been called up on standby for England – but even the presence of four frontline pacemen could not persuade the county to abandon its reliance on spin.

Trying to understand and agree with decisions taken at Kent over the years was never easy, but one event above all upset me more than most and that was the decision to sack Chris Tavare at the end of the 1984 season and to replace him as captain with Chris Cowdrey.

The saga began six weeks before the end of the 1982 season when Asif Iqbal agreed with a committee suggestion that he should stand down after six non consecutive years at the helm to give younger players a chance. For Pakistan Asif had been an inspirational leader during the seventies and had acquired a magnificent reputation. But by then with Kent he was beginning to tire of the everyday routine of county cricket and a change in captaincy seemed long overdue.

I am sure that over the years Kent has only really been happy when there has been a Cowdrey in the side and the committee were clearly anxious that Chris should have the job, but there was a major problem in that he had yet to firmly establish his position in the team and was clearly inexperienced for the job. The committee, however, decided that for the rest of that summer Cowdrey and Tavare should captain in alternate matches while their merits and capabilities were assessed.

By mid-September I was strangely convinced that, despite his age, Cowdrey was probably the best man for the task. During his handful of games in charge Tavare had hardly set the world on fire. Perhaps he did not feel sufficiently secure about his own future as captain to tell players exactly what he wanted and to stamp his own personality on the game. On the other hand Cowdrey, even as a youngster, was such an outgoing and confident individual that he did not consider holding back on anything. The committee, however, acted cautiously and went for Tavare, the older man, knowing that Cowdrey had plenty of years ahead of him in which to develop his cricket and leadership skills, and to establish his place in the side which was probably the only reason why he did not get the captaincy then.

Tavare is a much maligned and misunderstood character especially in the eyes of cricket followers around the world who have dubbed him the most boring Test batsman since Trevor Bailey. That reputation was born in 1981 when he was called up by England to face the Australians in the fifth Test at Old Trafford to fill the batting position at number three which no one else wanted. With England desperate for stability at the top of the order he made 69 first time around, followed by a seven hour stay for 78, including the third slowest 50 (304 minutes) in Test history.

The following winter in India, when Geoff Boycott abruptly returned to England from Calcutta, Tavare was pressed into action as a makeshift Test opener, a position he was to occupy for two years. But at Manchester and in the following months he was under orders to get his head down and defend and leave the stroke playing to the likes of Ian Botham, David Gower and Allan Lamb. It was not and never had been his natural game and it was not popular with the paying public. But Tavare played out the role because it was demanded by England and I never heard him complain. The real pity of the situation was that he never showed at international level the range of strokes he possessed. I accept that in Test matches the general level of bowling is much higher than it is in county cricket, but for those who have not seen Tavare in full flow for Kent I can vouch that he hits the ball as hard as anybody.

91

Tavare's quiet and reserved nature also carried through to the England dressing room where Ian Botham mischieviously nicknamed him 'Rowdy', but it was the thinker in him that appealed to me when he took over at Kent. Whatever the public's view of the man, as a team mate and captain, he was to me one of the straightest guys I had ever met, and a great bloke. In his two years as captain he thought very deeply about the game and was very good at communicating his wishes. In a way he was like Mike Brearley – he would always think a lot about a player's problems before saying anything, and then whether it was a cricketing matter or a personal problem affecting one's cricket, he would speak up with a lot of common sense.

Over the two years that Tavare was in charge my neck injury occurred and I did not play at all under him in 1984, but it still came as a bitter blow when he was summarily sacked at the end of the summer. The axe fell shortly after we had been beaten by Middlesex in the NatWest Trophy final at Lord's and many people felt that was the reason for his dismissal. He was publicly criticised for taking Derek Underwood out of the attack just as Middlesex were beginning to struggle in their search for 233 for victory. Derek had conceded only 12 runs in nine overs, but our pacemen failed to keep the lid on the opposition batsmen.

It might be my own blind faith in the man but I am sure that Tavare felt he had a very good reason to take Underwood off – he probably felt he was better equipped than some others to come back and bowl the rest of his overs later in the innings – and in any event surely one bowling change was hardly a sufficient reason to sack him. I believe that he would have been removed at some stage or another whether we had won the final or not. Some of the committee had clearly wanted Cowdrey to have the job and I reckoned he was going to get it eventually, even if Tavare had taken Kent to a string of titles each summer.

By the time I had recovered from my neck operation and was fit to play first class cricket again Cowdrey – the opposite of Tavare in many ways since he acts more on impulse, waves his arms more on the field and is prepared to take much more of a gamble to try and win matches – was in charge. But I returned to the Kent scene in 1985 still simmering with rage at the way the county had treated me the previous summer, during my long period of convalescence.

Money was again at the heart of the matter. Since I had been on England duty when the neck problem had arisen in Pakistan in 1984, I was led to believe I was entitled to a £200 a week insurance payout from the Test and County Cricket Board, for being temporarily and totally disabled. My view was that I was entitled to the cash as compensation for loss of earnings at international level but Kent decided the money should be theirs even though they had not contributed to the premiums. Although while I was in hospital various county officials had visited me and said I was not to worry about a thing, their idea of being considerate did not reach far where money was concerned.

When I went down to Canterbury to visit the other players in pre-season training I was left with the impression that Kent wanted their hands on that money and that I could be out of a job if I didn't agree to their wishes. It was Catch 22, since they knew that no other county would employ me while there were strong doubts about whether I would ever be fit enough to play again. Although I sought legal advice and was told I would probably win if I went to court, I was warned it would be an expensive gamble, so I backed down.

Kent tried to cushion the blow slightly by coming to an agreement whereby my salary was reduced by £200 a week so that I received the insurance money tax free and they also agreed to pay me my share of the team pool money for the season and my pension contributions, but I was still left several thousand pounds worse off than had I been playing for England. And that hurt even more when rumours began to appear that what I regarded as my entitlement was then used to go towards paying for the services of Alderman.

Despite all that had happened around me I was still keen to play for Kent at the start of 1985, but during that summer life began to become intolerable. For a start I was struggling to regain my form and confidence after a fourteen month break from the game, but Kent's idea of man management left a lot to be desired. I did not take many wickets early on, had a few niggling injuries that were fortunately nothing to do with the neck, and I needed help and encouragement from Cowdrey and the committee to pull through but it didn't arrive.

The situation with Cowdrey was always uneasy because I had made it clear from the start that I was a Tavare man and was still aggrieved by previous decisions. Nevertheless I sought Cowdrey out, told him how I felt but then added, quite rightly for the good of Kent and its supporters, that despite my feelings I would go out and try my hardest at all times and give the captain my full support. But as the season grew older we began to argue quite often and sometimes heatedly about the way I was getting on and the next thing I knew I was put into the second eleven.

My last wicket for Kent as Paul Prichard is trapped lbw at Folkestone. (*Adrian Murrell*)

That was the last thing I needed. For someone who had played Test cricket all over the world playing second eleven games in front of three men and a dog on a deserted ground came as a bit of a shock. I played two games – against the Army at Woolwich and Sussex at Dover, but it was useless. For a start I found it very difficult to get motivated and if my bowling was going to improve again I needed to be back in action against top class batsmen. The whole situation called for tolerance and understanding from Kent but it was not forthcoming.

It would have helped if there had been someone in a position of responsibility to whom I could have turned for advice, but I found it difficult to talk to our manager Brian Luckhurst about the position I was in. I had always thought that a manager in county cricket should act as a go-between with the players and the committee but in Luckhurst's case he seemed to me to be a committee man to the core and even though he might have been prepared to listen to players' views in the dressing room it was felt he would never have promoted them in front of the Kent committee if they did not toe the official line.

The final blow for me in 1985 arrived when Kent decided to sack Graham Johnson after he had given the county twenty-one years of loyal service. Apart from the fact that I was married to his sister-in-law I had always been close to him even before I met Helen. Like me he possessed a fairly weird sense of humour which I enjoyed and we often travelled and roomed together on away trips. While the other guys in the team would rush straight up a motorway from one ground to the next at the end of each game we used to take our time sharing the odd beer and jokes at a pub en route.

The true story of Graham's sacking has never been told but for his sake I want to put the record straight and because it illustrated just how Kent did treat some of their employees. Graham had decided not to take his usual employment in South Africa during the winter and was looking for a job in England that might possibly lead to a career outside the game, though he had no specific plans to call it a day at that time. But he approached the committee to discuss his future.

Kent later revealed they had decided that Laurie Potter should be groomed as a second spinner and during Kent's game at Chelmsford Graham was asked to retire, even though the county admitted that he was still capable of making their strongest eleven. The committee claimed they were planning for the future, though they should have known that Potter himself was not happy with the club and in fact chose to move to Leicestershire at the end of the summer.

After a meeting with the committee Graham agreed to retire and said he would prefer not to play again that season since he would find it hard to perform at his best knowing that his playing days were at an end. He did however assure Kent that he would keep himself fit for the rest of summer in case either Potter or Derek Underwood got injured. On that understanding he was even given permission to go away with his family for a couple of days.

Although Graham was not expecting to play again except in an emergency he was immediately selected for a Sunday League game against Yorkshire at Scarborough from which he withdrew since he was not in the right frame of mind to give of his best. Kent reacted by

And my penultimate innings for the county as I am stumped by David East off David Ackfield. (*Adrian Murrell*)

ordering him to play in our fixture against the Australian tourists saying that some of the other senior players wanted the game off and that the county's youngsters were needed at Edgbaston for the final of the Under 25s competition. Although it was finally decided that he would not play Graham agreed to go to the ground since no one knew that he had been ordered to retire and his absence might have aroused suspicion. He didn't even take his kit with him and after Kent took the field with Luckhurst in their side the *Mail on Sunday* ran a story saying that 'he had refused to play'.

The next day Luckhurst was surrounded by the press looking to follow up the story and after hasty discussions with the committee he announced that Graham had been sacked. They never mentioned the fact that he had been forced into accepting early retirement or that the county had agreed that he should not play again that season, they simply adapted the story to suit the situation.

Despite his treatment Graham turned down big money offers from newspapers to put his side of the story but the way he had been so shabbily treated after giving twenty-one years of loyal service affected my way of thinking. By the end of the season when I was playing in the second eleven and needing help, I thought there was little chance of a younger man like me getting it, if Kent were prepared to deal with a senior player like that. Being so unhappy with the set-up I decided I might be better off elsewhere and asked to be released from the remaining twelve months of my two year contract. True to character the committee turned my request down out of hand and it was a very miserable fast bowler who boarded the plane to spend the winter of 1985–86 in South Africa.

Towards the end of the summer I had gone over to Chelmsford to play in a benefit match for Graham Gooch and some of the players suggested that there was just a chance that I might have gone to the West Indies despite the fact that I had taken only 27 wickets in 16 games for Kent. To be frank the thought had never really crossed my mind since I had struggled to hold down a place in the county side. Although in some ways the words of the Essex lads were comforting they were also slightly harmful because until the side to tour was actually announced in September I harboured thoughts of being chosen.

In the end it was probably a good thing that England decided against gambling on my form, since the winter I spent in Natal was to prove a major turning point in my career. The initial approach to return to South Africa came from John Lever, who had just been appointed manager of Natal's Currie Cup side after spending the previous two winters, during which he was banned from England, playing for the State. Although Helen and I had enjoyed our two previous trips to Johannesburg we wanted to visit other parts of South Africa and grabbed the chance of seeing somewhere different. I was also quite keen to go to Durban since I knew most of the Hampshire side would be there and I had come to enjoy their company over the years.

Lever's initial approach, however, left me in some difficulty because Dr Ali Bacher, one of the most influential members of the South African Cricket Union, also rang up and insisted that he had a job available for me playing for the Orange Free State which had just been elected to the Currie Cup competition. When I pointed out Natal's approach he became fairly stroppy. Although he was insistent that I should go to the Free State he was not prepared to discuss a salary or conditions until I said 'Yes' and finally he gave me a twenty-four hour ultimatum to make up my mind. I simply 'phoned him later saying I was going to Natal. That I did not like his bullying attitude was one reason for the decision but also I didn't fancy the thought of spending the winter at inland Bloemfontein, which is the heart of Afrikaanadom, when I knew I could be by the sea in Durban. Later I learned that Bacher had responded to the snub by spreading the word among Natal officials that I was useless as a bowler, awkward to handle and unlikely to complete a full Currie Cup season because of injuries – it was a pleasure to prove him wrong.

I suffered though. Because of what Bacher told the Natal Cricket Union they only paid me basic wages and while I also played for Glenwood Old Boys I was pretty broke throughout the winter. I had to be overdrawn at the bank to the tune of £3,000 just to get by but the gamble proved worthwhile and I owe a lot to John Lever for that.

In the months that followed John Lever changed my whole attitude towards cricket and bowling in particular. Lever never tried to take me aside on the pitch or in the nets to suggest adjustments to my technique – it was in the bars of Durban over various glasses of beer that he changed my mental approach. Mixing with my 'team manager' during that winter was never a hardship. I had known him for a long time, admired his tremendous achievements for England and Essex and over the years enjoyed his company socially. No one was happier for him than me the following summer when the selectors called him back at the age of thirty-seven to play in the second Test against India at Leeds. Although he started nervously he went on to take six wickets in the match and I felt he should have kept his place for the third Test in Birmingham, but the selectors insisted it had only been a one match choice because he was best suited to the conditions at Headingley.

Our bar stool conversations about cricket tended to fall into two categories. Firstly he involved me in some of his decision making as manager – he would put forward an idea, listen to my thoughts on the subject and sometimes include them in his policy when it was later put to the team or captain. For the first time in my career that made me think far more deeply about the game. He would also talk about his own attitude towards bowling in general and the tactics he used against certain batsmen and gradually it began to rub off on me. With Lever always available as a companion in the background I started to look forward to playing again.

Mind you we have not always been so serious together. I remember one match for Kent against Essex when they were clearly planning to declare at the end of the day's play. With five minutes to go I had four wickets under my belt and John was batting. Since getting five in an innings is always an achievement and they were going to declare anyway John just stepped away to leg and let me have a free bowl at the stumps. I never forgot the gesture and later that same summer when by coincidence the roles were reversed I too stepped aside . . . that doesn't happen too often.

Just watching and listening to Lever I learned a lot and despite Bacher's reservations I had a successful season with Natal. In six Currie Cup games I took thirty wickets even though the Durban pitch was not the most helpful. In the days when Natal could call on Vince Van Der Bijl the Kingsmead wicket was barely distinguishable from the outfield and had been nicknamed 'The Green Mamba' by a succession of South African players because of its venomous reputation. Those days are now long gone, but with a new approach to the game thanks to Lever, I did not let the conditions worry me.

Thirty wickets in the winter may not seem a lot, but bearing in mind my meagre haul for Kent the previous summer it was like a windfall – furthermore if those performances could have been repeated during a twenty-four-match county programme it would have been like taking 120 wickets in a summer though I would have been pretty tired at the end of it.

In club cricket it was all slightly different. My job at Glenwood involved playing at weekends when I was free from my commitments with Natal and helping to organise the midweek coaching sessions. Sadly because the club players were not professional and merely playing as a hobby the response to my efforts was not great – I could not force players to do more than they wanted. But that said it was happy club and some of things that went on had to be seen to be believed.

But with Natal my confidence gradually increased and together with my new mental approach to the game I suddenly believed I could go out and give batsmen hell again for the first time in years and felt sure that I could also get good players out. I know that playing just six first-class games in the winter had hardly been very taxing but they were to prove to be vital stepping stones on the road back to the top.

9

Return to the Fold

F uelled by the newly instilled confidence that had been bred by my
  spell with Natal I had two main priorities when I reported back in
April 1986 for Kent's pre-season training. The first priority was to
establish myself back in the county side and the second was to regain
my Test place and although my future at the county was by no means
settled I was determined to put all those problems at the back of my
mind and concentrate purely on cricket and much to my relief it took
barely two weeks of the season before I was back in the headlines for all
the right reasons and to quote the old cliche 'nudging the selectors
again'.

For only the third match in our championship programme we
travelled across the Thames to play Kent's arch rival Essex who
throughout the eighties had been constantly collecting trophies while
we were ending each season empty handed. There was nothing like a
match with Essex to motivate Kent players and once I saw that the
Chelmsford wicket was likely to prove helpful I was raring to go.

In our opening fixture of the summer against Northants on a
typically dead Canterbury track I had only got two victims, but given
assistance I was able to prove that my winter of hard work had all been
worthwhile. It was the second hat-trick of my career that made the press
sit up and take notice and my victims were hardly in the rabbit class.
Keith Fletcher edged a catch to second slip and from the next two balls
Alan Lilley and David East presented wicket-keeper Steve Marsh with
two chances off the edge. I finished the match with six wickets, while
Terry Alderman took nine offering further proof, if ever it was really
needed, that on the right sort of surfaces Kent did have the bowlers
available to dismiss even the best county sides.

When you have been playing first-class cricket for a number of years
you are quite able to gauge what sort of form you are in and although

the season was still young I felt full of confidence as I drove away from Chelmsford at the end of the game. I felt I was bowling better than I had ever done and that it would only be a matter of time before the England selectors recognised the fact. Furthermore rumours were around that David Gower and Mike Gatting, who had been his vice-captain in the West Indies, had begun to make discreet enquiries about me.

It did not take a genius to work out why they were interested since the Caribbean tour had done little to solve England's shortages on the pace bowling front. Welshman Greg Thomas had not made the impact everyone had hoped for on his first overseas tour, Les Taylor had only been regarded as a stopgap, and Richard Ellison had lost much of the swing that had destroyed the Aussies only ten months previously. While Neil Foster had played in three Tests and performed creditably, vacancies were there for the taking and I could not see a great deal of opposition around – of those pacemen who had not toured the West Indies Norman Cowans seemed to have disappeared from the Test scene and Gloucestershire's David Lawrence was still lacking in experience.

Being picked for the one-day internationals against India gave me a great deal of satisfaction but not half as much as my first ball back in the England side after an absence of two years and three months. My victim was opening batsman Krishnamachari Srikkanth, an old adversary from my winter tour to the sub continent in 1981–82. Being naturally an agressive player, Srikkanth makes most bowlers feel they have a chance of getting his wicket at any time and he likes to hit hard from the start, and that was his downfall that day at the Oval. He attempted to drive without moving his feet across and presented Paul Downton with an offside catch behind. Sadly we lost the match by nine wickets, but by picking up two more victims in the second contest at Old Trafford I felt sure I would be in the twelve named for the first Test.

Just as Lord's had provided an historic setting for my county debut eight years earlier so it was to cricket's headquarters that I travelled for my return to Test cricket. But to be totally honest I did not put up a performance of which I was terribly proud as we lost the game by five wickets. My total haul for the match was six for 174 in 44 overs but my first innings bowling was not up to scratch. I took 4 for 146 as the Indians chalked up 342 to earn a first innings lead of 48 and afterwards freely admitted that I had conceded 30 or 40 runs more than I should have done which proved the difference between the two sides. But my own problems were submerged at the end of the match by the selectors

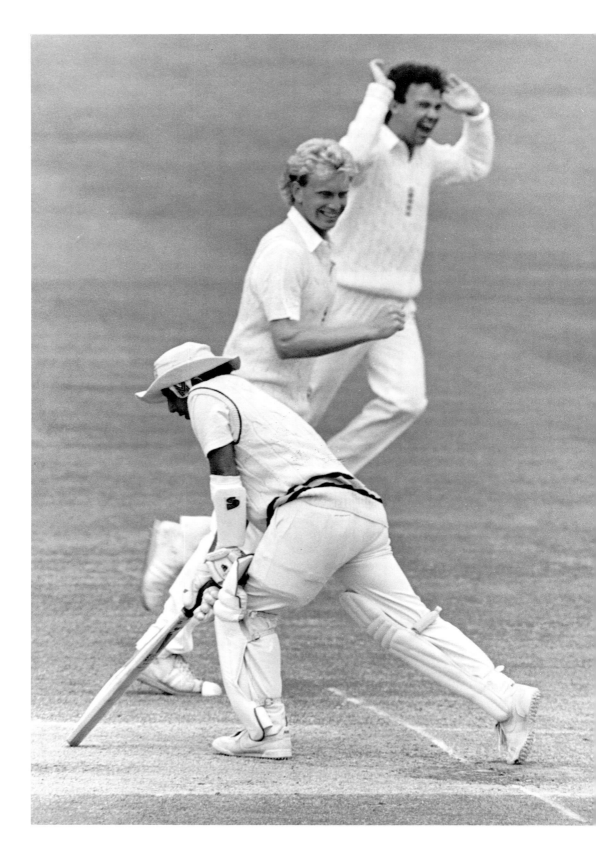

decision to sack Gower as captain and replace him with Gatting –
Lord's must be a graveyard for England leaders since Botham had met
the same fate there five years earlier.

I felt sorry for Gower because I did not think Mike Brearley, for all
his magnificent skills as a captain, would have prevented the West
Indies winning the previous winter's series five–nil because there was
such a class gap between the two sides. Twelve months earlier Gower
had been hailed as a national hero after taking England to victory over
India on tour after losing the first Test under trying circumstances in
Bombay. He followed up by thrashing the Australians in the 1985
Ashes series. He was only given the first Test against India at the start
of 1986 on a trial basis which was hardly fair to him and certainly did
not help the dressing room atmosphere at Lord's. The selectors had put
us all under extra pressure since we knew that if we lost the chances
were that Gower would be for the chop. That could not have happened
to a nicer bloke. I had yet to meet a cricketer who had not had time for
Gower, his manner had been so pleasant over the years that people
warmed to him automatically, yet his fate was cruel.

That said I could not see a better replacement than Gatting. During
my tour to New Zealand and Pakistan I shared a room with him on
several occasions and he always talked a great deal of sense about the
game. I was looking forward to playing under him and although it was
to be a difficult summer for the England side it did not seem to affect
Gatting who remained a bubbly, 'up out of the trenches and at 'em'
type even when given extra responsibilities. Despite my own
reservations about the way I had played at Lord's I was very much
hoping to be picked for the second game of the series at Leeds.

I thought I would have Gatting's backing because he had sensed the
new drive and ambition in my game. He knew that if he wanted me to
bowl a long spell, uphill and into the wind I would do so without
question, which had not necessarily been the case in my younger days.
And while I was prepared to react that way I thought Gatting would
stand by me. I was well aware of how Cowans had got on with him at
Middlesex and realised that anything less than one hundred per cent
effort would not be acceptable.

England lost again at Headingley but I was more satisfied in myself
taking 3 for 54 in India's first innings and I was beginning to get a

Always glad to see the back of Sunil Gavaskar – a triumph at Lord's. (*Adrian
Murrell*)

ABOVE: One of the strangest dismissals of all time: Graham Gooch catches
Maninder Singh at the second attempt, having dropped the first and having the
rebound flicked back to him by Bruce French. (*Patrick Eagar*)
OPPOSITE: My favourite study of me in action – at Lord's against India. (*Adrian
Murrell*)

series of favourable reports in the press when they once again found an
excuse to describe me as 'injury prone'.

Everything went wrong the night before the third Test at
Birmingham. I had reported fit and well when the team, as usual,
gathered at midday at Edgbaston on the eve of the match for a net
session and there was no hint of anything to come that night at the
England dinner in the Plough and Harrow Hotel. At two o'clock in the
morning, however, I awoke with a raging toothache and found it
impossible to get back to sleep. Three hours later I went down to the
hotel reception and got hold of some panadol, but they still didn't do
the trick and by early morning I was knocking on physio Laurie

105

Brown's door and he made hasty arrangements for me to see a dentist.

As I left the hotel Gatting was having his breakfast and his first reaction was 'God Picca you look bloody awful' but I still had faint hopes of making the 11 am start. But the dentist soon diagnosed an abscess on the nerve of my tooth and what little energy I had left after a sleepless night quickly evaporated as I spent an hour in his chair being hacked about. The match was only forty minutes from getting underway when I arrived at the ground and much though I wanted to play I was still in a lot of pain and not fit to take the field. Gatting accepted my apologies and Worcestershire's Neal Radford was given his England debut – the press however were not so forgiving. They were not impressed by an England fast bowler pulling out with toothache, when in fact it was nearly a month before I finished having treatment – and I don't recommend anyone having the root of a tooth drained when extraction is available – and my mouth returned to normal.

With the Indian series lost everyone was hoping that England's fortunes would be revived in the second series of the summer against New Zealand though I remembered from our clashes with the Kiwis on their own territory in 1984 that they would certainly not be the pushover that the public had come to expect. The point was quickly proved as we lost the opening one-day international at Headingley. Worse still was to follow as we quickly moved onto Old Trafford for the second match of the series.

After an England bowling performance that was best forgotten (I conceded 55 runs myself in only nine overs and others fared little better) the Kiwis scored a massive 284 for 5 which incensed the packed Manchester crowd. So much so that the England team was booed off the field for probably the first time since the 1933 Bodyline series in Australia. Although there had been times during my career when I had been verbally attacked with jeers and boos by a crowd I had never known it happen to a complete team before. The public was clearly running out of patience with England's losing streak and the selectors were not helping the players' confidence by constantly chopping and changing the side. That day however there was a silver lining around the clouds as Bill Athey played the innings of his life to score a brilliant 142 not out and earn us a victory against all the odds.

Here comes another Gorilla Hug – Ian Botham helps me celebrate the dismissal of Martin Crowe. (*Patrick Eagar*)

106

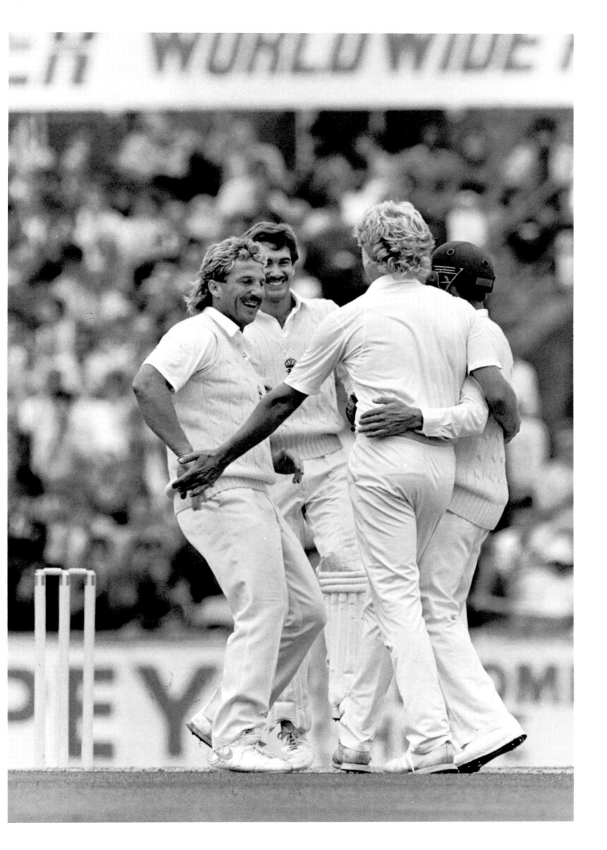

Despite pulling out of the Birmingham Test against the Indians, my instant recall for the Texaco Trophy games had only confirmed my growing belief that I was becoming established in the England side but it was vitally important for us all to capitalise on our shock win over the Kiwis in Manchester when we met up again at Lord's for the first Test. At least we managed a comfortable draw and with figures of three for 82 from 35 overs in the New Zealand first innings, and a quick victim at the start of their second I was personally quite satisfied.

But my body was beginning to show signs of strain after virtually two years away from persistent pressurised action and during a match at Leicester between Tests I began to suffer from sore shins which are the bane of fast bowlers' lives. At the end of the county game I had a quiet word with Gower, who, although he was no longer England's captain, was in a good position to tell me how the selectors would react if I missed the second Test at Trent Bridge. He suggested I 'phone Peter May direct and I was quite relieved at the way he reacted. After thanking me for my honesty May told me cheerily to go away and get myself fit again, a task I easily achieved in time to be picked for the final Test of the summer at the Oval.

The fact that my name was included again when the selectors announced their twelve for the game meant very little to anyone. The press and the public were only interested in Ian Botham's return to the international arena after serving the ban imposed on him by Lord's after he publicly admitted in a signed article in the *Mail on Sunday* to having smoked marijuana – ending a legal battle that had begun in Pakistan some two and a half years earlier.

Botham lived up to the expectations of a packed crowd when, after a new ball spell from myself and Gladstone Small, he produced an outswinger with his first delivery and Bruce Edgar obligingly edged a catch to Graham Gooch at slip. The size of the headlines grew even bigger as Botham followed up with the wickets of Jeff Crowe and Jeremy Coney and little notice was taken of my own return of 4 for 92 as the New Zealanders were bowled out for 287. Despite brilliant centuries from Gower and Gatting the game ended in a weather-ruined damp draw extending England's run of Tests without a victory to eleven.

Returning to Kent for the last few matches of the championship seemed much of an anti-climax and I found it hard to keep myself motivated after the thrill of returning to the England set-up and the large amount of overs I had bowled. It showed in a game at Trent Bridge where I asked Chris Cowdrey just to let me bowl virtually non-stop from one end. I hadn't particularly got the energy to do so, but it was the only way I could get through the game since I had found it so tedious in the field. It was not exactly a professional gesture, but it was all I could think of at the time. By the end of the summer, however, I had achieved all my goals and being established back in the Test side my bank manager was happy too.

If I needed any convincing about my England performances that summer it was to come in Australia on tour in the winter. A statistician from Melbourne produced a booklet early in 1987 which dealt with all the Tests played throughout the previous year across the world. A table of the leading wicket-takers showed me in fifth position behind Malcolm Marshall, Richard Hadlee, Imran Khan and John Emburey. But while the off-spinner had taken thirty-three wickets to my thirty-two in the year, he had played in thirteen Tests to my seven and bowled almost three times as many overs which spoke volumes for my strike rate.

10

Winning at Last

After twelve months in which very little had gone right for the England team I felt that there was considerable pressure on us all to succeed when we left Heathrow early in October 1986 for what was to be my second major tour in Australia. To restore public confidence back in England we knew we had to retain the Ashes which had been ours since 1985 and preferably win them again outright. To lose the precious urn would be the ultimate disaster because Australian form over the corresponding period – they had lost Test series at home and away to their neighbours New Zealand – had not exactly been full of glory and the critics had cruelly labelled the Ashes series that lay ahead as 'The battle for cricket's wooden spoon'.

For my part there was a desperate yearning to be a member of a winning England side or any winning side for that matter. I had experienced little success with Kent over the years and despite seven years of Test cricket had only been in a victorious England side once. That was the historic Headingley Test of 1981 and memories of the joy of that triumph had long since blurred into the dim and distant past and I was anxious to experience it all over again.

In the light of my performances the previous summer against India and New Zealand for the first time there was no real element of surprise when the name G. R. Dilley appeared on the TV screens in September as part of the squad of sixteen. In fact I was hardly surprised at any of the names except that, having played against Nottinghamshire in one of Kent's last county championship fixtures, I had felt certain that the selectors would pick both their openers, Chris Broad and Tim Robinson, with Bill Athey who had done the job in the final Test against New Zealand at the Oval as their understudy. Certainly I felt that Robinson, who scored 490 runs at an average of 61.25 against the 1985 Aussies had the edge over Wilf Slack whom I had regarded as an outsider for the tour. Sadly for Slack it was to be a most unfortunate tour, but Athey and Broad were to become our heroes in the months that lay ahead.

For once though the cricketers were not the sole focus of public interest. Since the whitewash in the West Indies the previous winter there had been much debate inside Lord's and the papers about the make-up of the tour management team with calls from all sides for a much higher profile in attitudes towards discipline and practice.

Since I had not been in the Caribbean, though I had heard plenty of rumours, I didn't quite know what to expect but as events turned out I certainly had no quarrels with the final choice of Peter Lush, the permanent Promotions and Public Relations officer of the Test and County Cricket Board, as manager with Micky Stewart from Surrey as his assistant with specific responsibilities on the cricketing front.

Over the years playing Tests at home I had met 'The Ger', as all managers are referred to on England tours, on several previous occasions. Although I would not say that I knew him well in advance of the tour he had always seemed a happy sort of guy and though he would probably agree that his knowledge of cricket, having never played at first-class level, was not too hot, he proved to be the right man for the job. Apart from his administrative capabilities he was also a tough negotiator for the best possible deals and conditions for the players but more importantly, for the first time in my experience, we had someone widely practised in cricket's press and public relations – a vital ingredient for the job.

The previous three winter tours had been sheer hell for some of the older members of the English team, who had been hounded around the world by newsmen not interested in cricket but purely seeking to tarnish the game's image. It was important to our hopes for success that we had a happy relationship with the press so that the players could relax at the end of a day. On all overseas tours there is always a large contingent from Fleet Street flying in the same planes and living in the same hotels and it had always seemed crazy to me that Lord's had never taken a more positive attitude. For an Australian tour, with so many Aussie journalists on the circuit as well, it was going to be necessary to have someone totally capable of dealing with press enquiries twenty-four hours a day, seven days a week and of the cricket administrators available in England Lush was the most qualified.

He also went on the tour armed with wider powers on press–player relationships which had been written into our contracts for the first time. While any reporter wishing to interview a player had to get prior permission from the manager we were not allowed to refuse 'reasonable requests' from papers once that permission had been granted.

When I first read the clause I was slightly wary since I did not fancy being hauled out to meet the press after a particularly bad day in the field. As it turned out the reporters only wanted to see the players who had done well each day and after a quick five minute chat we were free of all our obligations. In the early weeks of the tour Lush went out of his way to explain the ground rules to both the Australian and English pressmen and once they had been accepted a fairly good relationship was established with the team which was to last throughout the four and a half months we were away and Lush must take most of the credit for that.

It was during those early days that Stewart set out his own stall on the cricketing front. England had been slated in the Caribbean for what had been widely dubbed as holding 'optional practice sessions', but Stewart soon made it clear that his would be a tougher line. Although I would not say our training in the first week of acclimatisation in the steamy heat of Brisbane was any more strenuous than I had found on previous tours it certainly was different.

Instead of the normal stints of running followed by endless nets Stewart had gone to the trouble of devising different types of exercises and games to try and keep us all interested in the job in hand and although it seemed strange it was far more interesting to take part in practice sessions where we were playing rugby and football rather than simply cricket. It was also unusual to have an assistant manager shouting and bawling at the players to do as they were told. Although we quickly christened Stewart 'Hitler' we understood his early attempts to assert authority – it was proposed by the Test and County Cricket Board that he should be offered a three-year contract as England's manager if the tour went well. However it must be said that some of the players, used to a more sedate way of life in county cricket, where you are either left alone or quietly praised when something is done right, found it hard to adjust.

It was not for me to upset the apple-cart so I refrained from mentioning to Stewart that I slightly disagreed with him on the way he chose to handle my preparations for the gruelling itinerary that lay ahead of us.

In our first warm-up game against a Queensland Country XI, played in Bundaberg the home of Australia's famous rum, I bowled seven no-balls in my first six overs and it attracted some attention. To me, however, it was no new phenomenon. Since the county season had ended in mid-September I had been doing nothing – in fact after a long hard summer I had been deliberately idle – so it was natural that I was not one hundred per cent match fit when the tour started. I didn't have any intention of being so because I had at least been involved in all the one-day internationals and Tests during the summer and I needed time to recharge my batteries. I am sure other players felt the same especially those who had been in almost constant action since the tour to the West Indies had begun the previous January.

Since I was easing my way back into action it did not surprise me that for the first couple of weeks on the tour I struggled to find my bowling rhythm and during that period no-balls were bound to be fairly prevalent. In all the early matches I spoke to the umpires and asked them to keep a special eye on my overstepping and they were all helpful. It did not worry me when they said that I was consistently two or even as much as six inches over the line with my front foot, because all that would require was a little adjustment once the more important games began. I would have been more concerned if my foot had not been consistently landing in the same place, but that was not the case.

The situation seemed to worry Stewart, however, and he insisted that I spent several sessions in the nets, with Ian Botham acting as an umpire, to try to correct the fault. It served no immediate purpose because I have never been an enthusiastic net bowler and it was not until the second innings of our final warm-up match against Western Australia in Perth that I actually felt things had worked themselves out. To a certain extent Stewart and I also disagreed about my batting. I had finished the summer in fairly good form with Kent, but once he started talking about the way I was holding the bat and playing shots I started to think about what he was saying and all my form went out of the window. Stewart was doing a great job with some of the players but in my case I would have been happier to be left alone again.

In the month leading up to the Brisbane Test I gradually cured the no-ball plague and I was in a good frame of mind by the time we returned to Brisbane for the first Test though reading the Aussie papers it was clear that we were the underdogs. We had even been written off by the *Australian*, Rupert Murdoch's upmarket newspaper which screamed a headline at us saying 'Poms on Way to world's worst'. It was an assessment based on the poor performances of our batsmen in the three state games we had played leading up to the Ashes and also on

In action at Brisbane. (*Adrian Murrell*)

the Australians' own form on a tour to India which had just ended. In three Tests over there Allan Border's side had drawn twice and produced only the second tie in the history of Test cricket at Madras.

My thoughts on our chances nosedived when we lost the toss and Mike Gatting signalled from the centre of the GABBA pitch that we would be batting first. There was a chorus of 'Oh nos' around the England dressing room and I joined in having been convinced earlier that our one chance had been to bowl first and try and get the Aussies out for under 150 while there was still some early life and moisture in the wicket. When Chris Broad got out in the ninth over with only 15 runs on the board my fears worsened but fortunately Bill Athey, picked by the selectors for the Test with only marginally better form behind him than Wilf Slack, played a brilliant innings of 76 that not only put us in a strong position, but also, looking back, set the tone for England's batting for the rest of the series.

For the whole of that rain-shortened day Athey simply refused to try to play any shot that might have given the Australian bowlers an outside chance of his wicket and with the other batsmen taking their cue from him the first skirmishes in the Battle for the Ashes were ours. We had been warned that the Aussies left arm pairing of Bruce Reid and Chris Matthews was going to be the big danger to us, but with Mike Gatting making 61, David Gower 51 and later Ian Botham, a brilliant 138 we astounded the critics by reaching 456 all out.

Word had reached us prior to the game that the Aussies really fancied their chance of winning at Brisbane, but the odds had switched dramatically by the close of the second day when Phillip DeFreitas, on his debut, nipped in with the early wicket of David Boon.

Twenty-four hours later we had the Australians running for cover after rolling them over for 248 and enforcing the follow-on with a useful lead of 208. It must have been a shattering blow to Border's men after all the pre-match build-up they had been given and although our batsmen had come up with the goods at just the right time, I was not totally surprised. When the tour party had been first released it was not hard to spot the English players who thrive on the big-match atmosphere. People like Botham and Gower have never been overfond of net practice or less important state games played in front of small crowds. They needed the tension and importance of the Test scene to bring out the best in them and both had responded accordingly.

I knew how they felt and others had seen it in me before. Alan Knott once said to me 'Picca, you are a Test match bowler'. He did not

Heroes of the first Test win at Brisbane; with John Emburey and Ian Botham.
(*Adrian Murrell*)

necessarily mean at the time that I would always be good enough to play for England merely that playing at the top would be more likely to bring the best out in me. Looking back I would like to think that my approach and preparation for the Test series had been just right. I felt sharp when we went into the game, my rhythm was smooth and I got my reward by finishing with 5 for 68 in the Australian first innings.

It was a special performance for me. After seven years in and out of the Test side I had waited a long time for my first five wicket haul and it was shot back at those who had said I would never make it. Even during the summer when I had been bowling well against India and New Zealand Peter May, the chairman of selectors, had said in one newspaper interview that he wished England's strike bowlers would show more penetration and at last I had supplied the answer. But it was

116

a close run thing. I already had four wickets in the bag when Reid edged me to slip and Gatting dropped a not too difficult catch but minutes later Jack Richards tumbled to gobble up a low chance and suddenly I was England's hero.

I barely had time for a shower and a beer at the end of a long hard day before the press gathered outside our dressing room and Lush came in to tell me that I was wanted for an interview. It all felt very strange because over the years I had seen many players hauled out before reporters after a game but none had ever asked for me before. When I sat down in front of the cameras it was me who actually asked the first question. 'It's all new, what should I say?' I enquired. I managed to stumble through and then it occurred to me that even below England level, I had rarely been in a Kent side that had asked the opposition to follow on.

The timing of the rest day in Brisbane – it came after the third day's play – was crucial and strengthened our prospects. All the English bowlers then had twenty-four hours in which to regain their strength before having a second go at the Aussies and I just stayed in bed and slept throughout the break, while their batsmen had the same amount of time to fret about their fate. In the event we were held up by Western Australia opener Geoff Marsh who scored a fighting 110 before he was finally bowled by DeFreitas. We had seen plenty of Marsh in an earlier state game and I was pretty impressed as he had also scored a century against us then. Talking it over with Gatting he said he was not so convinced of Marsh's capabilities and he pointed out that Marsh possessed just three scoring shots. But our problem was that while we found it tough to get him out, he simply kept picking up runs with those shots and it said a lot for the guy's concentration that he rarely tried to play anything differently.

Thanks to his efforts and 45 from Greg Ritchie the Australians managed to avoid an innings defeat, but with only 77 needed to win England easily wrapped up the match shortly after lunch on the fifth day. As the final runs were struck I was completely overcome with emotion having waited so long to be on a winning side once again. The first person I sought out for a victory hug was our Scottish-born physio Laurie Brown since it was also his winning debut after twelve months handling the England side, following the retirement of Bernie Thomas.

Since I had also suffered such a long losing streak we had often joked in the past that one of us must have had a jinx on the England side, but

117

at last it had been broken. While Gatting was later beseiged by the press I just sat in the dressing room quietly shaking my head and trying to take it all in. My reaction had nothing to do with the fact that the Australians, so cocky before the game, had been hammered. For all I cared it could have been India, Pakistan or Sri Lanka – all I had ever wanted was to be part of a victorious England side. With the full cooperation of the management our victory celebrations at Brisbane's Crest Hotel lasted long into the night with endless bottles of champagne and there were plenty of thick heads the next morning for our short flight down the coast for the game against New South Wales at Newcastle.

To say we again performed badly would be an understatement as we went down by eight wickets after being bowled out for just 82 in the second innings. The press in Australia tends to be parochial and their reporters had a field day suggesting that our win at Brisbane had just been one big fluke. But Chris Broad and Bill Athey quickly provided the answer when we won the toss and batted first in the second Test at Perth. Their 223 run opening stand virtually put the match out of Australia's reach on the first day – though it needed centuries from David Gower and Jack Richards later on to take us to 592 for 8 declared. Although I accounted for Boon cheaply early on Australia's young-all-rounder Steve Waugh, who made a stylish 71, and Border, with 125, took the Australians to 401 in reply. The fact that we were unable to enforce the follow-on and that the match later ended in a draw was not our fault. The wicket on which we had batted so easily was never going to turn into a brute overnight and we did well to come within nine runs of forcing them to bat again. My own contribution was 4 for 79 from 24.4 overs and I was beginning to bowl with such confidence that I felt nearly every ball was capable of taking a wicket. Late in the game Mike Gatting was heavily criticised in some quarters for not declaring England's second innings until minutes before the start of the final morning when he set the Aussies a target of 391 in a complete day's play.

That looked at first to be a good decision when my opening delivery had Boon caught by Botham at slip, but in the event the Aussies did not have too much difficulty playing out time. Spinners John Emburey and Phil Edmonds bowled 55 overs between them in that innings but although there were cracks in the WACA pitch, when the ball hit them it did too much to cause any damage and for the rest of the time the conditions were ideal for batting.

The papers raged against Gatting but I agreed with his every move. Under such placid conditions a more generous declaration might just have left the Aussies with an attainable target. Even then had they reached about 180 in mid afternoon with only a couple of wickets down they might still have gone all out for victory and we would have paid the price for a rash attacking gesture. Gatting would never have been forgiven by English fans had we lost the Perth Test and in doing so thrown away the massive advantage in the series gained by our magnificent win at Brisbane. When a side is one–nil up in the Ashes in Australia no one but a fool would give the opposition even the slightest chance to climb back. As it was the Australians left Perth knowing that they had to win two of the three remaining Tests to regain the Ashes, while we could afford to lose one to keep them in our hands since a drawn series would be good enough.

I was happy to be rested for the four-day game against Victoria at Melbourne and while the break did me a power of good it gave the tour selectors a chance to have a good look at Gladstone Small and Neil Foster, who as it turned out would later play important roles as the tour neared its end. They did themselves proud with Small taking eight wickets and Foster six as England picked up a six-wicket victory.

Some people have said since that the third Test at Adelaide was one of the most boring for years, but looking back it was a very good yardstick for us to measure our confidence as a team. We might have been rocked by a rib injury which struck Ian Botham during the Perth Test and put him on the sidelines. And our heads could easily have dropped as the Australians batted throughout the first two days to reach 514 for 5 on a typically flat South Australian wicket, but thoughts of defeat never occurred to us. Again it was Athey and Broad who showed the way, confirming that the track was full of runs by putting on 112 for the first wicket and there were thoughts in the dressing room that we could go on to make 700 and possibly win by an innings if the wicket should turn for our spinners on the fifth day. Sadly our middle order did not perform at its best and it needed a ton from Gatting to make the game safe.

In getting only two wickets in the match it was one of my lowest international returns of the year but there were good reasons for that. With Botham injured the selectors, without another all-rounder on hand, were forced to call up either a specialist bowler or another batsman. Being ahead in the series they quite naturally decided to give James Whitaker his first Test appearance bearing in mind that the

A large coffin for the Ashes. (*Adrian Murrell*)

more runs we could get on the board the less likely we were to lose the match.

But that also meant there was increased pressure on the four bowlers in the side to do the job normally carried out by five. I know that Gatting had taken 4 for 31 in the game against Victoria as a preparation to bowl in the Test, but there were still just four of us in the frontline. I know that had a negative effect on me when the Australians batted first and I am sure the same went for DeFreitas as well. As strike bowlers we would normally expect to bowl flat out for a short spell at the start of a day, return again at fairly regular intervals and hope to be able to bowl another spell shortly before the close with a new ball. But with no other specialist seamer available DeFreitas and I knew we were in for a couple of days hard work and I am sure it took the cutting edge of our deliveries since we felt we always had to keep something back in reserve.

In the end I bowled 32 overs in the Australian first innings and found myself suffering from a swollen knee which kept me out of the state game against Tasmania that followed. I could have played and would have done so had the selectors decided they wanted me, but instead it was felt that I should rest. What upset me, however, was that the press had been told about the problems with the knee.

I had been having slight trouble with fluid in the right knee joint since the first Test at Brisbane but it had never been a major problem up to that stage. I was quite able to do all the bowling that England required provided that during the lunch and tea intervals Laurie Brown and I packed it with ice and I took regularly the anti-inflammatory tablets which he prescribed. I don't think anyone who watched the first three Tests would argue that I had been bowling better than ever for England despite the injury.

By missing the state games between the Tests the fluids had subsided and as far as I was concerned there was nothing to worry about, but I have always been twitchy about injury stories right back to my first tour of Australia seven years previously – ever since missing the last Test of that series people had been saying that I was injury prone.

This time around I did have a problem but I was bowling well and carrying it successfully and at a time when I deserved a bit of praise I did not want to give my critics ammunition that would overshadow my achievements. Furthermore I was not the first fast bowler in history to take the field less than totally fit. In the past decade Dennis Lillee, surely the greatest fast bowler of all time, had rarely taken the field without some minor ailment – the day to day pounding up to the crease had taken a heavy toll on his body. The same had applied to me for years since I had long accepted that minor niggles were part and parcel of the fast bowling profession.

11

A Very Festive Season

The knee was still playing up when we arrived in Tasmania for the final state fixture of the winter and since it was not a vital match for me the tour selectors and I agreed that rest would be the safest bet. We all had three strenuous weeks ahead of us with the Melbourne Test starting on Boxing Day, the America's Cup Perth Challenge opening the New Year and the Sydney Test soon after that, so there was no point in risking more serious damage. For me Hobart's Wrest Point Casino Hotel was aptly named though I did venture onto the tables at night, finally breaking even at roulette and blackjack on our last day in Tasmania.

Our overnight trip to Canberra two days before Christmas to play against an eleven raised by Australia's cricket-mad prime minister Bob Hawke took on far more significance than the tour planners could have possibly foreseen. Instead of enjoying a leisurely day out in Australia's administrative capital the fifty-over contest proved to be a fitness test for both Ian Botham and myself. Botham had not played since breaking down at Perth and although he only bowled off eight paces his ten overs for 42 runs, with two wickets, was sufficient to suggest he had a role to play in the forthcoming Test at Melbourne. I fired in six overs straight off with the new ball, but my knee did not feel comfortable, my line was all askew and suddenly there were doubts about whether I would be available.

Whatever my troubles there was no way I was going to allow them to spoil the festive season at the Menzies Hotel in Melbourne. Guests visiting there for the first time are prone to think they are in somewhere like Pentonville or Wandsworth since the interior is built like a prison – two long high blocks of rooms, each with a balcony, facing each other, with a glass roof and a long drop down into the bar area below. Foreboding it may have looked but the whole tour party was in high spirits; although we were still only one–nil up in the Test series, there

Queueing up to congratulate me after bowling David Boon at Perth in the second Test. (*Patrick Eagar*)

was a general feeling that after our performances in Perth and Adelaide there was no way the Australians were going to beat us. We were all aware there was a Test due to start on Boxing Day and that called for restraint on the booze front but it failed to stop us enjoying ourselves.

Ian Botham opened up his suite to all the players on Christmas Eve and with Elton John in attendance we had quite a lively party. Although we were all careful not to go overboard in the drinks stakes I have to confess to suffering from a slight headache when I awoke on Christmas morning and hardly felt up to attending the traditional champagne party thrown by the press. After a couple of glasses of bubbly, however, I was put in the right frame of mind for the rest of the day by a pantomime acted out by the reporters.

It was a tribute to the way Peter Lush had fostered relations between the press and the players throughout the tour that we all found their act pretty amusing. Their chosen subject for the ten minute drama was Mike Gatting's highly publicised sleep-in on the first morning of our game with Victoria in Melbourne. Titled 'The Big Sleep' it portrayed Mike, played by Dave Norrie of the *News of the World,* lying in bed surrounded by mounds of room service trays covered in food, having a nightmare about the possibility of David Gower regaining the England captaincy.

Anyone can oversleep on tour, particularly with an itinerary as gruelling as ours was, but it is not quite what the people at Lord's expect from an England captain. Still Gatting had weathered the storm a fortnight earlier and the mood was right, the time was right and the amount of mickey taking just right for the pantomime to be well received – even Botham was in stitches when the room service waiter said his next order was to deliver some coke to the 'greatest living cricketer'.

As the press party broke up Phillip DeFreitas and I returned to our room to prepare for the second traditional event of Christmas Day, the players' fancy dress lunch. On previous overseas trips they had always been exclusively male affairs with wives and girlfriends forced to eat elsewhere so that any player who had chosen not to bring his partner out to join him on tour would not feel he was missing out and become depressed. The rules, however, had changed in the three years since I had last toured and the ladies' presence made very little difference although the humour and language had to be toned down to allow for the presence of children.

As elected secretary of the grandly titled 'Players' Social Committee' I had been fairly deeply involved in the organisation of the party. My main task in the previous weeks had been to prepare charges for the Kangaroo Courts which had sat regularly to charge and fine players for ridiculous misdemeanours to raise money for the lunch. Players had been hauled up before the committee for the most trivial of offences but such was the justice of the proceedings that the more minor the charge, the bigger they were blown out of proportion and the fines were adjusted accordingly. Some examples of the hearings can never be released to the public but of the others physio Laurie Brown was done for ringing home and speaking to himself on his answering machine, DeFreitas was fined for referring to the Australian Premier Bob Hawke as Bob Hope while our overweight manager Peter Lush was frequently chided for claiming that he had actually passed the pre-tour medical.

The hefty amount of cash raised by the courts was all put towards the presents which the social committee had decided each player should receive at the lunch. Again some of the best examples are team secrets but Botham received a packet of grass seed, John Emburey a pair of underpants shaped for an elephant while my colleagues had decided I should receive an emergency cigarette held in a glass box for use only when I ran out of the free supply laid on by Benson and Hedges, our official sponsors in Australia.

Some of the fancy dress costumes were simply outrageous and highly imaginative. Although a lot of hard work went into their conception after the social committee had given each player a specific letter of the alphabet which had to be worked into a theme, finding the right gear in Australia with dress hire shops in almost every city was not as taxing a problem as it is say in India. My own plan was to get myself wheeled into the lunch on a stretcher with an intravenous drip of Bollinger champagne to imitate the famous laid back attitude of David Gower. Sadly the plan backfired since obtaining a stretcher proved a tough task and I ended up being pushed on a porter's trolley.

DeFreitas walked away with first prize after turning up as Diana Ross complete with a long dark wig and a clinging long red dress. In fact before he was even seen in public we tried to get him to shave off his moustache and planned to tell Wilf Slack that Ms Ross was in the bar downstairs waiting to share a Christmas drink. Unfortunately DeFreitas would not play ball to that extent though from the back he looked just the part.

As the party came to a close we all drifted back to our rooms for a quick snooze, but even though there was an important Test due to start within twenty-four hours we still had one other item on the agenda. The BBC had arranged through the Noel Edmonds show for us all to be linked up with our folks back home. Although I had particularly been looking forward to seeing Helen the whole thing was a complete disaster from start to finish. In agreeing to take part Peter Lush had insisted that we be included in the first part of the show so that we could all get off to bed, but we were kept hanging around for an hour and were unable to get away from the cameras until 11.15 pm, furthermore the sound and picture quality on the tiny monitors in front of us were so bad that the whole event turned into a farce. It was then that Lush demonstrated how there was no way during the tour that people were going to use his players and get away with it. After

125

two fairly heavy days celebrating Christmas he knew that we all needed to retire early and he wrote a strong letter of complaint to the BBC on our behalf.

As Boxing Day dawned and we all went early to the ground for practice there was still a lingering doubt over my knee. Although the fluid had subsided Laurie Brown had discovered I had damaged a ligament and felt I should take a late fitness test. It was a tough decision to make when Gatting came up and asked me whether I could play or not. In such cases I had always believed in honesty being the best policy and I told him that while I might have been able to start the match there was no guarantee that after three or four days that I would still be able to bowl. Some of the other lads moaned a bit when I pulled out, but in my own mind I was prepared to take their criticism and let someone else who was fully fit have my place – it was going to be a vital Test for England and there was no way I would risk breaking down and leaving the side a bowler short.

It took me about two hours of brooding to get over my disappointment but by then Gladstone Small and Botham had begun making deep inroads into the Australian batting. Small took 5 for 48 as the Aussies were bowled out for 141 by the tea interval on the first day and that served to confirm my view at the start of the tour that England had picked the right bowlers to do a job during the winter and even if Neil Foster had been selected to play I am sure he would have performed just as well.

Once again it was Chris Broad with his record-equalling third century in successive Tests who ensured we had a handsome lead of 208 on first innings. Before the tour began I hardly knew Broad, but since we were both tall and blond people in Australia had begun to remark that we could easily have been brothers and we formed a strong friendship – though I must say some of it was based on pretty harsh sarcasm and leg pulling. As a player, however, I had to admire his efforts on our behalf and he proved to be the find of the winter.

The speed with which Australia collapsed to 194 all out second time around with the match only three days old caught me completely off guard. I had been given the day off from twelfth man duties and had slipped back to our hotel because I am not the world's best watcher of games in which I am not involved. I listened to some of the play on the radio and after writing a couple of letters drifted off to sleep. When I finally awoke and turned on the TV I discovered that the Aussies had lost eight wickets and the Ashes were all but ours.

After swilling some water over my face I dashed into a taxi and finally arrived at the Melbourne Cricket Ground to see the last two wickets fall to give us victory by an innings and 14 runs. Small, who had waited patiently for his chance, had taken two crucial wickets at the start of the innings, including that of Allan Border, and was correctly voted man-of-the-match. Although he had been given my place I felt no jealousy as he had come in and bowled magnificently to help us clinch the series. While I had enjoyed the winning feeling that night in Brisbane, some six weeks before, it was nothing compared to the delight that day. At last I was part of a team that had achieved something and even had the rest of the tour turned into something of an anti-climax the main object of the winter had been achieved – the Ashes were ours whatever was to happen in the Sydney Test and the critics who had been so damning just two months previously had been hastily forced to rethink their words.

The scenes that followed in the England dressing room were remarkable with champagne being sprayed everywhere and talcum powder poured all over Tony Crafter, when the Australian umpire came in to congratulate us.

After an hour some of the Australians came in to join us and I felt for them after all the pressure they had been under for the previous two months, but it was only a fleeting emotion and I am sure that had the boot been on the other foot they would not have felt sorry for us for a moment.

It was over three hours later before some slightly tipsy English players started to emerge from the ground, but the celebrations had only just begun. Botham opened up his suite again and for the first time on tour we all let our hair down. Elton John, by then our most loyal fan, acted as disc jockey – though he only played one of his own numbers – and the partying went on all night. Time just vanished though had any of us consulted our watches I am not sure we would have been able to read them. By finishing the match inside three days, we had earned two extra days off in which to recover and with the Ashes in the bank the celebrations were fully justified.

I had first met Elton John in New Zealand three years earlier but to be honest I had never felt totally at ease in the company of someone so famous who had achieved so much. Big name cricket stars like Botham and Gower find it comes easily to them to rub shoulders with celebrities from other walks of life but I was in such awe of the rockstar that I constantly feared muttering something inane and silly to him.

127

That night, however, he was great. He kept coming over and saying 'we stuffed them' and I think he felt as much pride in our performance as we did.

Some of the hangovers were still raging by the looks on the faces of several players when forty-eight hours later we headed for Perth for the week of one-day internationals against Australia, Pakistan and the West Indies which had been arranged as part of the Festival of Sport being run in conjunction with the America's Cup. There was always the danger in our camp that after winning the Ashes the rest of the tour might be a let down. But at the same time our confidence in our own ability had grown and the tour management were determined that we should keep competing for the six weeks that remained of the tour.

Two years earlier Australian fans had certainly seen how victory in a Test series could have an adverse effect on an England side. In the early months of 1985 after winning a tough series in India 2–1 and putting up with all the hassles that surrounded the tragic assassinations of Mrs Indira Gandhi and the British Deputy High Commissioner in Bombay, England had gone down under for the World Championship of Cricket and performed lamentably. Stewart, however, informed the players in no uncertain terms that he did not wish to see a repeat performance.

Everyone fully expected the West Indies to pick up the $20,000 first prize in Perth. Since the Kerry Packer revolution they had been visiting Australia virtually every year and taking away almost all the prizes on offer. But in a talk with Gatting we had both reached a conclusion that they could be beaten provided we stuck to a rigid strategy that involved bowling a tight line just short of a length on the off stump at their batsmen. We had both looked back over some of their rare defeats and noticed for instance how Mohinder Armanath, hardly the most dangerous bowler in the game, had proved so frustrating and effective in the 1983 World Cup Final and had helped India pull a remarkable victory out of the bag.

My conviction that we could win in Perth, providing we played at our very best throughout, was strengthened on the 2,200 mile flight across the Nullabor Plain from Melbourne. The West Indies had begun their opening match against Pakistan while we were still in the air and about forty minutes flying time out of Perth news came over the intercom from the captain of our flight that Viv Richards' side was in great difficulty chasing a modest target of around 200. Later as news of the West Indies' defeat filtered through a great cheer went up from all the English team because already a path towards the final had opened.

Our opening game was scheduled for two days later against the Australians and by that time I did not give them a cat in hell's chance of beating us. In the Tests we had managed to establish such a psychological advantage over them that it did not matter to us whether we had to play them over one or five days. Once Mike Gatting had won the toss and Broad and Athey had done their job again with an opening stand of 86 we were on our way. Although Allan Lamb scored a fine 66 it was Botham who left everyone gasping for breath as from only 39 balls he smashed seven fours and two sixes on his way to 68. Having batted the other end from the great all rounder in that famous Headingley Test of 1981 I had plenty of first hand experience of his powerplay, but that exhibition in Perth was outstanding even by his own standards.

Botham's enemies have often referred to him as an uncultured slogger and for most ordinary mortals to hit the ball as hard as he does slogging is their only resort. But Botham is not like that. He has always been a very technically correct player and it says chapters for the man that he can still play by the text book while hitting the ball at an enormous velocity.

Defending a total of 272 was never going to be a major problem provided we kept to the important bowling discipline of line and length and our hopes soared in the third over when David Boon cut DeFreitas straight into the hands of John Emburey at gulley. From then on the Australians desperately needed one of their frontline batsmen to play a major innings and it came from Dean Jones. He made a brilliant 104 after being dropped at 16 by the skipper, but he never scored fast enough or had sufficient support to provide a major threat and we won by a comfortable 37-run margin. Although I had been wicket-less in my first spell back after injury, I eventually accounted for Jones when he chipped a catch to Gower at mid-off. When Ken MacLeay with a hard-hit 28 threatened a late Aussie revival I picked up a second victim when John Emburey took what was in my view the catch of the winter, tumbling backwards at deep long on. Finishing with 2 for 31 from my ten overs I was happy with my fitness again.

Two days later it was time for the crunch meeting with the West Indies and we all knew only too well that they would be smarting after their defeat against Pakistan. There was a certain amount of discussion inside our camp as to which course should be taken if the toss went our way. Over the years since one-day cricket became so popular it had become an established practice to ask the opposition to bat first because if there was going to be any life in a wicket it would be at the start of a game and as a bowler that held a great deal of appeal for me.

There was another big factor be taken into account at Perth. Since the match was a day/night fixture there was a lot to be said for avoiding forcing our batsmen to be at the crease during twilight when the massive new lighting pylons at the WACA would take over from natural daylight and dew would descend in the darkness to freshen up the pitch again. With the West Indies in particular it was felt that they might not be so strong when under pressure batting second and chasing a target – batting first and given a good start by the ever dependable Gordon Greenidge and Desmond Haynes they had always been capable of cutting loose in their natural Caribbean style and setting unreachable targets.

As it turned out when Viv Richards won the toss and chose to field first we were left without any options to consider. When Broad and Athey managed only one run between them against the pace threat of Malcolm Marshall and Joel Garner the nightmare of England's ill-fated trip to the West Indies ten months previously began flooding back into our dressing room.

But Allan Lamb has never been afraid to take on the West Indies pacemen as he showed in 1984 when he scored three Test centuries against all the odds and with him scoring 71 and Jack Richards an admirable 50 we eventually managed to reach 228 for 9. It was by no means a match-winning total but on the other hand at least we bowlers had been given something to defend. Our task was made easier by Small who accounted for both openers Greenidge and Haynes as he bowled his allocation of ten overs straight through and Botham helped a lot by conceding only 29 runs in his stint despite having to bowl mainly at his close friend and arch rival Richards. The history books will show in years to come that when I returned for my second spell I knocked the stuffing out of the West Indies middle order with four wickets in 22 balls. It was sufficient to earn the man-of-the-match award from Ian Chappell and fire England to a nineteen-run win, but to be fair I thought the honour should have gone to Lamb for his bravery at the crease, or even Small or Botham who had done so much to make sure the West Indies innings was kept in check early on.

I was certainly not used to all the credit that was being heaped on me from every side. For the first time in my career wherever I went I was being approached by Aussie and English fans alike and being praised for my performances. From always trying to be virtually anonymous I found myself recognised by waiters in restaurants, barmen in hotels and just ordinary people in the streets.

It would be a lie to say that sudden recognition did not give me a nice feeling inside but I was determined not to let it go to my head. Throughout my career up to that point I had experienced plenty of life's ups and downs and having known what it was like to be to totally depressed with the game I was not going to become wildly elated. Still it was nice of Gatting to say at one press conference in Perth that he thought I was bowling as well as any English fast bowler had done for ten years and while my first man-of-the-match award in England colours was an honour, it was an even greater feeling to know that we still had the winning habit as a team. The tournament organisers though were sick. They had hoped that the Australians and the West Indies would prove a crowd pulling attraction in the final but after Pakistan beat the Aussies as well, they were left playing their final qualifying match purely to avoid finishing last in the table.

I watched a bit of that game on TV in our hotel and realised just how hurt the West Indies looked in the shadows of defeat after winning so often in the past. After bowling a tight line and length against both us and Pakistan they immediately resorted to their standby weapon of short pitched bowling. Although the competition rules stated that any delivery which passed over a batsman's shoulder should be deemed a no-ball the West Indian pacemen did not seem to care about giving away the odd run if the effect was to scare the wits out of the opposition. So it was hardly a shock when the Australians were bowled out for 91 with the West Indies winning by 164, but it meant nothing to us because they weren't in the finals.

Our opponents were going to be Pakistan and we had an opportunity to have a good look at them first in our final qualifying match, the result of which was going to be immaterial. For the first time in the competition we were asked to bat second and with Shoaib Mohammad scoring 66 and Javed Miandad 59 their final total of 229 for 5 was certainly going to be no pushover. As a wise precaution against my knee playing up before the final I had been rested from the game, but it was a sad evening for Neil Foster. Given a rare opportunity to play an international game on the tour he had suffered injury after bowling only four overs. Victory was virtually ours once Broad and Athey put on 104 for the first wicket in just 27 overs and although there

was a bit of panic in the middle order Emburey and DeFreitas, batting sensibly, saw us home with two balls to spare so we went into the final with a one hundred per cent winning record and with a morale boosting victory over our opponents tucked in the belt.

After quite an exciting dress rehearsal it was a pity in a way that the final should have turned out to be a one-sided affair. While winning was of paramount importance to us and we achieved our goal with almost clinical efficiency, the game itself was a complete let down for the fans who had paid to watch an even contest. Only Javed Miandad with 77 stood up to our bowling attack, shepherding his tail well, as we limited the Pakistanis to 166 for 9 from their 50 overs, for which I will take some of the credit since I had a tight return of 1 for 23 from my ten overs.

For virtually only the second time on tour our openers failed to do their job as both Broad and Athey were back in the pavilion before the fourth over had been completed with only seven runs on the board. But when a side has a middle order which reads Gower, Gatting, Lamb, Botham there is so much match-winning potential that hope is never lost until they have all departed. Their combined experience steadied the ship and as Gatting led the way with a top score of 48 we sailed to victory and the trophy with just under ten overs and five wickets to spare.

Again an England team that had been written off when the tour began had triumphed by putting a second trophy in the bag and we knew we had every chance of clinching the World Series Cup later, though the West Indies would be going flat out for revenge.

Only one event soured the taste of our victory champagne in Perth and that was reports in some papers that a group of English fans had started a mini-riot after the game. This was blown totally out of proportion since a total of twenty-eight arrests on the day hardly compared with the seventy or so made on the opening day of the Melbourne Test and there was no guarantee that all those who spent that night in the cells were England followers. In fact I had found their support throughout the four matches in Perth welcome. They may have been waving their flags and chanting some soccer-style slogans but when we were so far away from home it made a refreshing change to have people on our side – some Aussies are so partisan that they are

It takes a lot to unsettle Allan Border, but its always worth a try. (*Patrick Eagar*)

abusive when an opposition fielder cuts off a four on the boundary, instead of applauding an athletic piece of fielding as we would expect at a match in England.

After the presentation in front of the main stand in Perth I was quite happy along with four of the other lads to take the trophy over to our fans who were all gathered at the far end of the ground. It may have been seen by some as a soccer Cup Final type gesture, but they had been standing a long way from the ceremony and deserved to see what we had won after giving us such magnificent support. More than that however was the fact that for some years now England supporters have been paying hard earned money to travel overseas and watch us play only to have to put up with the frustration of seeing us lose. This time, however, they had supported us well in our moments of glory and I felt it only right that we should make some gesture of thanks. Although some commentators felt our action might have incited trouble after the game, the police actually praised us for trying to take the heat out of what could have been a nasty situation. A quick change and it was back to the hotel for more champagne . . . need I say more.

12

A Unique Treble

Obviously with the Ashes already firmly in our hands there was a certain amount of anti-climax surrounding the fifth and final Test of the winter at Sydney. Yet we went into the game full of confidence and determination because we wanted to finish the series without suffering a defeat and a final scoreline of two–nil or three–nil would have been ample to keep our critics silent. It seemed like a desperate measure to us when the Australians called up an unknown off spinner in the form of Peter Taylor. The thirty-year-old agricultural scientist from North Sydney had only played a handful of first-class games and had not even been mentioned earlier when we travelled to Newcastle to play against New South Wales, in fact I doubt whether he was even on the ground, but it was to turn out to be an inspired choice.

Having proved my fitness again during the week in Perth I fully expected to get back into the side for Sydney, though I would have understood, despite any disappointment, had the selectors decided to stick by a winning Test team. Certainly Gladstone Small, who replaced me in Melbourne had done more than enough to hold his place and in the end Phillip DeFreitas was left out. That in itself may have been a bit of a gamble but I felt fit and more than backed by my own ability to do the job in hand.

Small and I each managed an early breakthrough when the Aussies won the toss and chose to bat first as I trapped Greg Ritchie leg before and Small beat Geoff Marsh off the pitch resulting in a catch to Mike Gatting at slip. But the Australians nevertheless fought back to reach 343 mainly due to Dean Jones scoring 184 not out. It was a superb innings but we were all left wondering what score the Australians might have got had it not been for one umpiring decision. When he was five Jones appeared to glance Small down the leg side where Jack Richards completed a tumbling catch. But Tasmanian umpire Steve

Champagne and beer all the way in Australia. (*Adrian Murrell*)

Randall turned down our frantic appeals and we had to live with the consequences. Umpires all around the world can make mistakes and more often than not they are accepted without a murmur. Randall was unlucky to be in Sydney, with its multi-million dollar TV screen cum scoreboard where within seconds of any decision the players are able to turn around and see the replay.

Small, however, came up with the goods for the second match running, finishing with 5 for 75 and considering that no one else apart from Jones scored more than 34 we were reasonably happy with their total. But then we all experienced a big shock as Chris Broad, Bill Athey and Mike Gatting all failed at one time when our innings got underway and it only went to emphasise how well they had done in the previous four Tests and how much we had come to rely on them.

A first innings deficit of 68 took some of the sting out of my bowling when the Aussies batted second time around. Knowing that we would be chasing a target on the final day with the wicket taking increasing amounts of spin, I settled for accuracy rather than strike power after accounting for Geoff Marsh early on. As if to underline the way different players had contributed at various times previously on the tour John Emburey chose Sydney for a career-best Test performance of 7 for 78. The wickets followed hard on his fighting 69 in our first innings and our vice-captain fully deserved the success. Despite his five wickets in the opening Test at Brisbane, the many overs he had bowled since had yielded very little, but he kept our target down to 320 in a shade over seven hours.

Unfortunately the spinning combination of Taylor, who by now we realised was not the worst off spinner in the world, and Peter Sleep made sure we toiled all the way and although Gatting produced a captain's knock of 96 we were finally bowled out with only seven overs of the match remaining. Losing by 55 runs left us all slightly shattered, though the knowledge that we had already won the series cushioned the blow slightly. But the victory had a remarkable effect on the Aussies. For weeks they had been taking considerable stick from their own press who are totally unwilling to accept failure. But victory in Sydney restored belief in a lot of their players and as we faced up to them in the final three weeks of the tour in the World Series Cup we suddenly found an opposition that was far harder to beat. We were all tired but there was just enough energy left in the camp to mount a challenge for the unbelievable treble and our enthusiasm was increased slightly by the challenge of a different sort of competition.

Our first obstacle though was the weather as we headed for Brisbane, for the third and final time on the tour, and flew straight into a heatwave. It had been hot on all our previous visits to Queensland but by mid January conditions were only just bearable and given the general fatigue of the side it was not surprising that they took their toll. I have to query whether it was just by coincidence that England, the weariest of the three teams involved in the WSC had been drawn to play two games over that weekend – Australian TV knew full well they would be on a winner if the eventual final were to be between Australia and the West Indies.

Whatever the hurdles, however, we got off to a flying start on the Saturday with our second successive win over the West Indies and for the second time I was named man-of-the-match, though it was really a combination of Dilley and DeFreitas that did the damage. Dangerman Gordon Greenidge went in the second over lbw to DeFreitas, but it was the eleventh over of their innings that put us on top. Richie Richardson edged me to Ian Botham at slip and next ball I was convinced I had Viv Richards trapped in front of the stumps. He survived that appeal but the next delivery nipped back off the pitch and bowled him off the inside edge. Although Desmond Haynes and Gus Logie put together a stand of 86 the West Indies never quite recovered and their total of 154 was passed with some comfort thanks to 49 from Chris Broad and 46 from David Gower.

The Aussie papers the next day were full of inquests into the West Indian demise and most blamed the advancing age of some of their players, but I think it went deeper than that. Looking at the side they took with them to Australia it was noticeable that the number of batsmen with a grounding in county cricket had been reduced considerably. Apart from Greenidge and Richards none of them had vast experience of conditions where the ball moves around a lot and all our bowlers were certainly doing that. It helped us particularly in the WSC matches where, with a new white ball used at each end, there was still some shine left for both DeFreitas and me when we returned for a second spell at the end of an innings.

Sleep came easily to most of us after that victory. The temperature had gone well over one hundred degrees during the day and we were all shattered yet within twenty-four hours we were back at the GABBA facing the Australians who had enjoyed a few days rest after the Sydney Test.

Overnight the Brisbane wicket had lost a bit of its moisture and with tiredness making motivation difficult for our players the Australians piled up 261 for 4 with Jones scoring his second century against us in a week. It was a sign of the Victorian batsman's growing confidence that was to stay with him throughout the competition. Of the new breed of Australians he seems to have one of the brighter futures, but before his stature in world circles is confirmed he will have to prove himself again after going through the odd patches which can affect all batsmen since confidence plays a large part in his game. Considering the heat we did well to get within 11 runs of the Australian total, but that was mainly due to 111 from Bill Athey, who was clearly suffering from heat exhaustion when the match ended. His concentration was brilliant but no one stayed around long enough at the other end to see us home.

'Surely its meant to be a pat on the back captain!' (*Adrian Murrell*)

Our chances of qualifying for the WSC finals increased in midweek when the Australians lost to the West Indies in Melbourne and we travelled to Sydney for a cliff-hanging victory over Allan Border's men with Allan Lamb scoring 18 off what surely must have been the most dramatic last over of all the winter games. Although I got two wickets in that match there was a significant new approach from the Aussies as they paired Geoff Marsh and Dirk Wellham together at the top of their order and on a flat wicket neither DeFreitas nor I had been able to forge an early breakthrough, which had been so instrumental in some of our earlier one-day games. Still Lamb's 77 not out was just another example of how often during the tour different individuals had produced match winning performances at different times, proving that we were not a one or two man band.

With England playing two matches in Adelaide over the long weekend that traditionally marks Australia Day we knew that two more victories would take us into the finals and we got off to a great start on the Saturday with our third successive one-day win over the West Indies. The old firm of Athey and Broad set us up with an opening stand of 121 and with John Emburey taking four wickets Viv Richards' team failed to get within 89 runs of our 252 for 6. Had anyone suggested before the tour began that we could beat the West Indies in three games, let alone three on the trot, I would have told them to wake up to the realities of life, but our confidence, already so high, seemed to be growing even more.

Sunday saw the West Indies bounce back to beat Australia, but then suddenly our form deserted us as we crashed to the Aussies by 33 runs on the bank holiday Monday. It was to be the first of three defeats that almost cost us our place in the finals. At a subsequent press conference Mike Gatting laid the blame at my feet and he did have a small point. As the Australians reached 225 for 6 I dropped Allan Border, who was to make 91, when he was still in single figures, allowing them to recover from a dreadful start that had been inspired by three wickets from DeFreitas. It was a simple skier to mid-on but somehow I just misjudged it. Several kind pressmen suggested later that the sun must have been in my eyes, but there were no excuses from me, it was a big boob and we paid the penalty. Though I was disappointed I think Gatting was a bit strong when he called it the turning point, because I didn't even play in our next two defeats.

On the Monday in Adelaide I put my shoulder out while throwing in the outfield and while I completed my ten overs with the ball, the second spell was painful and pretty ineffective. The injury was still troubling me when we reached Melbourne for games against the West Indies and Australia within the space of three days. Before each of those matches Laurie Brown gave me a fitness test but things were not quite right. Although I felt happy when bowling, as soon as I attempted to throw the ball in the field the shoulder played up and I had to tell Gatting there was no guarantee that I would be able to complete ten overs if I played.

The situation had not improved by the time we flew to Tasmania for the final qualifying match with the West Indies. With three defeats behind us it was a match that we had to win to reach the final where Australia were waiting for us. The night before the game we had a team meeting at the Sheerwater Country Club. Amid suggestions that we had run out of steam the tour management and Micky Stewart, in particular, urged us to have one last try. I guess some of the players already had their sights set on an early flight to England and their families, but the pep talk had the desired effect.

There was some moaning in the dressing room after I failed yet another fitness test on my shoulder and some people felt that I should have risked the injury for such a vital match, but I argued that it would be better for me to rest further and be available for the finals provided we got there and it turned out to be the right decision, though I felt an element of frustration. With Chris Broad scoring a stubborn 76 we reached 177 for 9. It was not a convincing total, but from our previous meetings with the West Indies we knew we could make them struggle if they were put under pressure early on, especially since their long standing openers Greenidge and Haynes were both absent because of injury.

As it turned out we beat them by 29 runs thanks to a magnificent performance from all our bowlers, but particularly from DeFreitas. Although he got the early wicket of Richardson it was his second spell that clinched the game for us. When he returned to the attack for the forty-third over the West Indies with four wickets in hand wanted 46 to win and with Jeff Dujon still at the crease a tense finish could have been on the cards. DeFreitas wrecked their hopes, however, by conceding only eight runs in his first three overs back in the attack and the grand slam was within our reach.

That performance from DeFreitas showed astonishing discipline from a twenty-year-old and convinced me that he has a bright future for England, providing of course that he is left to develop at his own pace and not put under pressure to succeed all the time. During the tour I had shared a room with him on a number of occasions and had noticed that although he always appeared cool, but not cocky, in public there were times when self doubts crept in. Early on the tour he discussed his action with Stewart. Although his arm does get a bit low at times DeFreitas still manages to generate plenty of pace and bounce but in the early nets Stewart made some attempts to get his arm higher, and it clearly worried the youngster.

The difference of opinion produced some quite hilarious situations where DeFreitas would deliberately bowl with a flat arm in the nets and ask Stewart if things were any better, but eventually they reached an unwritten agreement, and from the way he performed on tour there could be little doubt that DeFreitas's action, while not from the textbooks, was pretty effective. But it was during the times when he felt unsure of himself that I took it upon myself to try and help out. I advised him that Stewart was likely to be around the England scene for a long time to come and that if he also wanted to be then he would have to make an effort to get on with England's first cricket manager. I had a vested interest in his development since two bowlers working well at either end help each other as well as taking the pressure off each other and I certainly appreciated some of his efforts. If in years to come DeFreitas takes my England place, though I would always back my own ability against anyone, I would like to think that some of the advice that I gave him turned him into a better player. By the time we flew home he had certainly handled the pressures of a first major tour overseas better than I had done at the age of twenty, seven years earlier.

As we left Tasmania and headed back to Melbourne for the first of the best of three WSC finals there was an air of confidence that having overcome the hurdle of the West Indies we could beat the Australians to take the trophy even though the opposition's level of confidence had soared almost daily since the Sydney Test. The night before our first encounter I was still worried about my shoulder but two conversations convinced me that I should play. After a team meeting both Gatting and Botham separately sought me out for a chat. They said that it was vital that I risk not being able to complete my overs and play because the Australians did not relish the thought of facing me. Although I had been desperate to return to the side it was just the sort of spur I needed. DeFreitas and I quickly had the Aussies in dire straights.

Tim Zoehrer – the Aussies' newest recruit as an opener – went to my third ball caught by Gatting at slip and in the second over the skipper also accounted for Geoff Marsh off the bowling of DeFreitas. Three for two could so easily have become ten for four as Gatting held onto a catch off Allan Border only to see me called for a no-ball and then Jones edged another tantalising close to first slip. Jones and Border made the most of their good fortune and while they were putting on 103 for the third wicket there was always the chance that the Australians might assemble a match-winning total but John Emburey bowled brilliantly at the death and we restricted them to 171 for 8.

The match, however, turned out to be a strange affair for two completely separate reasons. Firstly after rain had washed out the first hour it was reduced to a forty-four-over contest for entirely non-cricket purposes. Although Melbourne has six magnificent light towers, installed at a cost of many millions of dollars, the authorities were not allowed to extend play beyond the scheduled finish to make sure each side faced fifty overs. The moguls at Channel Nine TV insisted that their programme schedules could not be interrupted by a late finish, and despite a packed crowd the Australian Board had no alternative but to dock six overs from each innings. When one considers some of the trash shown on early evening TV in Australia I am sure most of the viewers would have preferred to watch a decent game of cricket.

The second event that had large effect on the outcome of the match was an astonishing display of power hitting from Ian Botham. In Devonport, England had decided to open with the all-rounder against the West Indies and although he scored only eight in that match the experiment was continued. The England innings was only fifteen overs old when Botham was out caught behind, but by then he had already scored 71 in an opening partnership of 91 with Chris Broad and the first final was virtually ours. The Botham experiment was based on getting him to the crease early and giving him the chance to play a long innings in a one-day game which had rarely arisen while batting at six and forced to slog as overs had run out. If ever in the future he manages to open and bat through fifty overs with the style he showed at Melbourne he would threaten every record in the history books for one-day totals.

As we moved onto Sydney for the second final our determination to finish the tour in style grew. None of us wanted the series to go to a third and deciding match in Melbourne for we all knew that if the trophy could be clinched in the second game we would all have three days off before flying home. But the result we wanted was by no means certain when, batting first, we only managed to score 187 for 9. It had come as a great shock to us when Broad, Athey and Gatting all went cheaply and it needed some sensible batting in a last wicket partnership between Bruce French and yours truly to push the total up that far.

The Australians juggled their order again sending out Border himself to open with Marsh, but the gamble failed. With both DeFreitas and myself bowling the meanest possible line and length we made runs hard to come by. While the Australian openers put on 55 for the first wicket it took them 19 overs and they fell so far behind the clock that the required rate was pushed up to over six an over. Although Neil Foster proved a bit expensive in two early spells, Botham kept the squeeze on with 3 for 26 in ten overs and Emburey was just as tight early in his stint. Only Simon O'Donnell offered any threat to us as he lashed both DeFreitas and Emburey for straight sixes late in the game and eventually we found ourselves in the position of having to prevent the Aussies scoring 28 off the last two overs.

Under ideal circumstances I should have bowled the fiftieth but the order had not worked out that way and Gatting knew Foster would have to bowl the last over, despite conceding 41 runs in his first nine. I tried desperately to keep O'Donnell quiet in the forty-ninth but still went for ten runs and with eighteen wanted off the last six balls memories flooded back of Allan Lamb destroying Bruce Reid under similar circumstances on the same ground a fortnight earlier. To the relief of us all, however, Foster, who had waited months in the wings for the chance to play an international match on the tour, only conceded nine runs and we were home and dry. But it had been so tense that during that last over I remember saying out loud 'come on we don't want to have to go back to Melbourne for a third game'.

As Mike Gatting went up to receive the trophy and deal with the press there was a strange, almost silent air in the England dressing room. It was a combination of players being stunned by achieving a unique treble and relief that four and a half months of gruelling pressure had finally come to an end. But everyone was ready for a big party that night, knowing that whatever the size of the hangover there was no more cricket to be played.

Although it was by no means certain in advance that we were going to avoid a trip to Melbourne for a third final Botham and myself had agreed to throw a party that night anyway. The team was no longer staying in a hotel, but in some luxury apartments at Bondi Junction and since Botham had insisted on the penthouse with a huge balcony

Chris Broad deserved a hug after his batting performances Down Under. (*Adrian Murrell*)

looking out over the city and I was sharing with him we had agreed it would be an ideal spot for a barbecue.

During our early conversations Elton John had been present and he decided to treat the lads. When Elton does something it is usually in style and he arranged for the caterers from the luxury Sebel Town House Hotel to set up the food. That was a slight disappointment to me since from my earliest days of visiting South Africa I had enjoyed cooking in the open air but in the end I was just happy to relax, helped by liberal lashings of beer and champagne that had been snapped up from the team room along with some wine donated by a company with which Botham had a promotional deal going.

The party went on late into the night, but contrary to reports it was a quiet affair. Later the *Sunday People* was to report that the fire brigade had to be called when the lifts in our block jammed in the middle of the night and that a girl had been seen running around the apartment dressed only in a bra. Sadly with the press there is always someone determined to put a damper on a moment of triumph and several people referred to that report when I returned home four days later. So to put the record straight I would point out that it was Dennis Lillee who got stuck in the lift and that was an accident. The lift had in fact been playing up for several days and had already trapped a businessman along with tour manager Peter Lush. We could hardly be blamed for it going wrong again in the early hours of the morning, furthermore the girl concerned had actually been spotted in a street outside the apartment block and since we were on the fifteenth floor any connection with our shindig was totally coincidental. It was not that sort of party, in the time before I went to bed at 5.30 am all that happened was that the players and a few friends sat around talking and drinking about the events of the tour.

13

New Horizons

Although during the summer of 1986 I established myself as an England regular for the first time and looked forward with confidence to being in the party to tour Australia, my relations with Kent had not improved appreciably. They had acknowledged my return to the Test arena by offering me a new two-year contract – it was more a question of added security rather than cash in the bank – but I had refused to sign it. I had a growing feeling, although it was only small to start off with, that I might still be better off getting away to another county and escaping all the hassles that had become involved in playing for Kent.

We were still not winning trophies under Cowdrey's leadership and there was a common theme in some dressing room conversations that referred back to how much easier life must have been at Kent in the seventies when we were winning all sorts of competitions. A few of us recognised that there was no real comparison since ten years previously Kent had been a far better side than most others around and it was natural they would be successful. In the intervening years other counties had made great strides forward and by that I don't just mean the fashionable ones like Essex and Middlesex – people used to look upon Glamorgan as an easy touch, but once they started signing good players like Javed Miandad and Winston Davis, and older pros like Mike Selvey and John Steele they were just as capable of beating any side on their day. Kent too had unearthed a whole generation of young players, but there were no easy games any more and it had become increasingly hard to meet the committee's expectations.

Then there was the question of loyalty. If someone is loyal to me then I always try to respond one hundred per cent, but the way I had been treated over the previous years had hardly convinced me that Kent were ever so keen about my playing for the county. It seemed more a question that I should feel honoured to be employed by them and accept all the flak that was around. I think they honestly believed that no player would ever turn his back on Kent and so when I left to tour Australia a part of me felt I should get away if only to shake the Kent system up, for the good of the other players I would be leaving behind.

I had refused to sign the new two-year contract which the county offered me during the summer because frankly the money side of it was less than I expected. Although I was an England regular and had been playing Test cricket on and off for seven years they were only prepared to pay me £9,000 a year. That sum was barely more than any newly capped county player, without international honours, could expect under the pay guidelines agreed between the Professional Cricketers Association and the Test and County Cricket Board. Again it seemed that Kent was not particularly interested in retaining my services.

At the same time my attitude had become slightly more mercenary. As a youngster I would have played first-class cricket for nothing but times had changed. I used to play cricket simply for the love of it, but having bought a house, got married, had one son, with another child due at the end of the tour, I had to think more about long term security. Although playing cricket just for the game's sake is an admirable principle it doesn't pay the household bills and the time had come when I wanted to earn enough to keep the bank manager happy.

Kent, however, was prepared to just sit back and play a waiting game. I am sure that the committee felt that my principles would not extend as far as leaving the county and throwing away the chance of a lucrative benefit in 1990, but at the same time my resolution to strike out for a better deal was growing. By the time I left with England to go to Australia a state of complete impasse had been reached.

It was to remain that way until December with absolutely no contact between myself and the club. All the time I was mixing with other England players on the tour I was getting the odd hint of the size of salaries they were earning and also some suggestions of the sort of figure I might be able to command if I decided to move elsewhere and steadily my resolve to get away grew. Had Kent just made some sort of reasonable gesture I would have signed. It may sound trite, but I needed to feel wanted.

But if I needed any convincing that Kent was unlikely to make any positive moves in my direction the proof came while we were playing the third Test against the Aussies at Adelaide. I had heard along the grapevine that Chris Cowdrey would be bringing a new contract out for me when he arrived in Australia before Christmas to undertake a six week coaching commitment. I expected him to make some sort of contact instead he arrived in Sydney and merely gave the letter to Allan Lamb's wife Lindsay who was to act as a courier when she flew to Adelaide to join up with the tour party.

There was nothing new in the contract, so I decided to make one last move before I was due to become a free agent under TCCB rules on 1 January. After the Adelaide Test the England party was due to fly on to Tasmania where my Kent colleague Richard Ellison was spending the winter playing Sheffield Shield cricket. Ellison and Cowdrey had been close friends, sometimes inseparable, especially since they had both been chosen by England to tour India in the winter of 1984–85. Knowing that the pair intended to spend some time together at Christmas, I met Ellison for a drink while we were in Tasmania and told him my position, hoping that it would get back to Cowdrey at a later date.

I do not know whether the message ever got through but there was still no contact as Christmas passed and on New Year's Day, while we were in Perth for the America's Cup Challenge I became officially unemployed at county level and free to listen to offers. The response from other counties was quite overwhelming. Again under TCCB rules they needed to give Kent a fourteen-day notification of their intention to hold talks with me and some were so anxious that they lodged their letters on December 17 just to make sure they could be first in the queue. Waiting for me in Perth were representatives from Lancashire, Hampshire and Somerset, while several other counties came on the phone from England.

Despite the massive interest, with one county prepared to offer me a long term contract at around £14,000 a year, I was reticent to make a snap decision until I had finally exhausted all hope of a reasonable settlement with Kent. But the chances of that happening disappeared when we moved on to Sydney and I had my long awaited opportunity to meet Cowdrey face to face during the final Test. The meeting did not go as I wanted and although there was no bitterness or harsh words Cowdrey did not think that Kent would agree to my demands. These were for a salary of £10,500 and a contract which would be long enough to ensure employment until my hoped for benefit in 1990.

Cowdrey promised to phone Kent on my behalf but was not optimistic and by then I realised my future would lie elsewhere. At the time Hampshire were the front runners for my signature. All along while considering which other county would suit my needs their name kept cropping up. I certainly didn't want to live in a big city, since it is not the ideal environment in which to bring up young children which ruled out the two big London clubs Middlesex and Surrey. And while Helen and I wanted to live in the country we 'didn't want to go somewhere that would be totally strange to us.

Hampshire fitted the bill nicely since we both had friends in the New Forest area, I had always got on well with their captain Mark Nicholas and what was more important I had always enjoyed the social company of his players. While Cowdrey was going back to Kent one last time and Hampshire was urging me to sign, I received an offer out of the blue from Worcestershire which literally staggered me.

At the time Duncan Fearnley, chairman of Worcestershire, was in Sydney to complete the signing of Ian Botham, who had decided to leave Somerset in the wake of the decision to sack his two big West Indian friends Joel Garner and Viv Richards, but I had no inkling that he was also interested in me.

At a specially staged press conference after play on the Saturday night of the Sydney Test Botham duly signed a deal that had looked on the cards since the end of the previous summer and afterwards he, his solicitor Allan Herd and several Worcestershire committee men retired to the bar at the team's hotel, The Sebel Town House, to celebrate in style with expensive French champagne.

It was in the next two hours that my fate was virtually sealed. A journalist friend of mine began to quiz cricket committee chairman Mike Jones closely on whether Worcestershire had any genuine interest in signing me as well and discussed the type of terms that might interest me. After that things moved faster than I could have ever imagined. The journalist rang me later that night to suggest a meeting with Jones shortly after the start of play the next day. It took just thirty minutes in the members' bar at the Sydney Cricket Ground to convince me that a deal could be struck and by the time I met up with Jones again during the lunch interval I was convinced. Actually it would be more truthful to say that I was staggered.

Although I have no intention of divulging the exact details, Worcestershire were prepared to pay me twenty-five per cent more than Kent in a five-year contract. At the same time Jones had opened negotiations with Carphone the Frome based company that had been

A warm welcome from Worcestershire fans as I make my debut against Kent at New Road. (*Patrick Eagar*)

150

instrumental in helping to finance Botham's move to New Road. The suggestion was that in return for a certain amount of promotional work for their company additional monies would be invested on my behalf.

The offer was irresistible and at the same time revolutionary. I suppose I was just fortunate to be in the right place at the right time. Apart from Jones, Worcestershire's chairman Duncan Fearnley was also in Sydney along with Graham Thomas and Ted Markwick, the chairman and deputy chairman of Carphone, who were able to handle negotiations on the spot without time-wasting phone calls back to London. For my part I was able to enlist the guidance of Botham's solicitor Herd, who is a redoubtable veteran in negotiating new cricket contracts.

The only important person not directly on hand was Helen who was back in Canterbury and heavily pregnant with our second child. That, however was not a major problem. From the start she had made it abundantly clear that she would support whatever decision I made about my future. I tried to keep her fully informed about all the developments but inevitably while I was on the other side of the world there were times when she did not quite understand exactly what was going on especially as events were beginning to move so fast.

Still at the back of my mind all the time were her words which said basically 'I don't mind where you choose to move to as long as we move together. I know that the two of us can be happy wherever we live.' Although it was not a vital factor in my final decision the deal that was being set up with Carphone also held a small attraction for Helen. Among the company's other sporting sponsorships was a connection with three-day eventing and since Helen had been involved with horses all through her working life, I foresaw there could be some additional benefits there.

Overall I was totally impressed with the way Worcestershire handled matters that weekend. At Kent and probably at most other counties the details would have taken ages to work out with constant referrals back to various committees. Jones, however, did not seem to acknowledge the existence of such red tape and by the time Herd flew back to England the following Monday he was armed with instructions to sort out my contract for a move to New Road.

Before I finally signed, however, I had to have one last meeting with Cowdrey, because even at that late stage I would have been prepared to stay with Kent had they shown any interest. Basically I said to Cowdrey

And a quick wicket as Neil Taylor departs caught behind. (*Adrian Murrell*)

that I had received a fantastic offer and that I hoped Kent would respond. I didn't ask them to match or better it, just improve their offer. In essence I said 'Look you turn around and say that you want me to play for Kent and prove it to me with a better contract.' I was still at heart a Kent player but I was not prepared to let loyalty stand in the way of financial security. I knew the county had invested money in me over the years, made me a first-class cricketer and turned me into a Test player, but none of that was going to pay the bills.

After my first meeting with Cowdrey in Sydney I had virtually

153

decided to leave and it was merely a question of deciding which of the eight counties that had shown an initial interest should be followed up. But when he held out virtually no hope of Kent changing their minds when we talked again my decision was made. Worcestershire had shown they were prepared to care for me and secure my future and I knew then that I owed them a lot. But there was another surprise in store for me.

I expected that Herd would take sometime in London sorting out the small print and our communications were hampered by a strike by Telecom engineers and we were forced to use Fax facilities. But then out of the blue after England had played the West Indies in a day/night game at Melbourne on January 30 I found message from Herd waiting for me late at night saying that he would be signing on my behalf – I had issued him with a power of attorney – within an hour. My first move was to inform our manager Peter Lush of my decision and although it had not occurred to me he advised that I should tell Kent before the move was released to the press.

Fortunately that proved quite easy since I rang the secretary David Dalby and there was no bitterness whatsoever as he wished me luck for the future. By then, however, it was well past midnight and I had to face the press at a hastily called conference. It was something I dreaded since I had never had to face reporters before about anything which hadn't actually happened on the field of play. But I was grateful to David Lloyd of the Press Association, Peter West (*The Daily Telegraph*) and Paul Weaver (*Daily Mirror*) for keeping questions down to a minimum and accepting basically what I had read out in a prepared statement. It was about two in the morning before I finally got away and was able to celebrate with a quiet bottle of champagne – knowing that months of uncertainty had come to an end.

I was not aware at the time that back in London there had been considerable debate in the papers about my proposed move with various cricket officials warning that it could open the floodgates to a soccer-style transfer market which could have an adverse effect on the game, but I did know the move was right for me.

For years counties have held almost a feudal grip on their players. While I accept that some clubs have not been able to pay their players more than the basic minimum agreed by the Professional Cricketers Association, they have always had a hold over their unhappy employees who have been forced to show a false sense of of loyalty with the hope of a lucrative benefit.

Another new arrival at Worcestershire. Our second son Christopher was born within hours of my debut much to the delight of Paul, Helen and myself. (*Graham Morris*)

The system of course had one merit in that a player around the age of thirty to thirty-five was given the chance to make enough money in a year to make himself financially secure for life. But it failed to take into account others, less fortunate, who might have been forced out of the game at a younger age without any lump sum, no formal training in any other profession than cricket and with little hope for the future. In the early 1980s the PCA attempted to get the benefit system scrapped and replaced by a type of insurance scheme for each individual, but the proposal had to be ditched because it did not offer a viable alternative.

With Worcestershire's help, however, I had been able to escape from a county where I was not totally happy with a scheme established which avoided the need for a benefit. In any event the idea of going round the county cap in hand for a whole year begging for money had never really appealed to me. I hope now that other discontented players reading this will accept that providing the right sponsors can be found at another county they too could contemplate finding a new club and a new challenge without being forced to spend years tied to their current employers just for the sake of a benefit.

I returned from England's tour of Australia to begin immediately the process of house hunting in Worcestershire and eagerly awaiting the start of a new season and a new chapter in my life. I was looking forward to playing with Ian Botham at county level, meeting up with my new county team mates for whom I felt there would be a great future because Worcestershire had made several strong signings in previous years and hoping that I would be able to give them one hundred per cent effort in return for all they had done for me – it was the least the county would deserve.

Looking back it had been an amazing winter. When it all began I was unhappy at Kent and the reputation of the English cricket team had been at an all time low. Yet five months later my personal employment problems had been settled in a way I never could have imagined and as a team we had stunned the cricketing world by lifting all three trophies that had been on offer on tour, and there was hope for a bright future on all fronts.

Index